Understanding School Refusal

of related interest

Nurture Groups in School and at Home
Connecting with Children with Social, Emotional and Behavioural Difficulties
Paul Cooper and Yonca Tiknaz
ISBN 978 1 84310 528 2
Innovative Learning for All series

Working with Anger and Young People
Nick Luxmoore
ISBN 978 1 84310 466 7

Bully Blocking
Six Secrets to Help Children Deal with Teasing and Bullying – Revised Edition
Evelyn M. Field
ISBN 978 1 84310 554 1

School Phobia, Panic Attacks and Anxiety in Children
Márianna Csóti
ISBN 978 1 84310 091 1

Listening to Young People in School, Youth Work and Counselling
Nick Luxmoore
ISBN 978 1 85302 909 7

Working with Parents of Young People
Research, Policy and Practice
Edited by Debi Roker and John Coleman
ISBN 978 1 84310 420 9

Helping Children to Build Self-Esteem
A Photocopiable Activities Book, Second Edition
Deborah Plummer
Illustrated by Alice Harper
ISBN 978 1 84310 488 9

Helping Adolescents and Adults to Build Self-Esteem
A Photocopiable Resource Book
Deborah Plummer
ISBN 978 1 84310 185 7

Self-Esteem Games for Children
Deborah Plummer
Illustrated by Jane Serrurier
ISBN 978 1 84310 424 7

Understanding School Refusal

A Handbook for Professionals in Education, Health and Social Care

M. S. Thambirajah, Karen J. Grandison
and Louise De-Hayes

Jessica Kingsley Publishers
London and Philadelphia

The authors and publishers are grateful to the proprietors listed below for permission to use the following material:
Figure 21.1 from p.264 in M. Atkinson and G. Hornby (2002) *Mental Health Handbook for Schools.* Oxford:
Routledge/Falmer. Reproduced with permission from Taylor and Francis Books Ltd.
Figure 37.1 from p.694 in D. Cicchetti, S.L. Toth and A. Maughan (2000) 'An Ecological-Transactional Model of Child
Maltreatment.' In A.J. Sameroff, M. Lewis and S.M. Miller (eds) (2000) *Handbook of Developmental Psychopathology,* 2nd
edn. New York: Kluwer Academic/Plenum Publishers, pp.689–722. Reproduced with kind permission from Springer
Science and Business Media.
Figure 8.2 from p.145 in R.W. Roeser and J.S. Eccles (2000) 'Schooling and Mental Health.' In A.J. Sameroff, M. Lewis
and S.M. Miller (eds) (2000) *Handbook of Developmental Psychopathology,* 2nd edn. New York: Kluwer Academic/Plenum
Publishers, pp.135–156. Reproduced with kind permission from Springer Science and Business Media.

First published in 2008
by Jessica Kingsley Publishers
116 Pentonville Road
London N1 9JB, UK
and
400 Market Street, Suite 400
Philadelphia, PA 19106, USA

www.jkp.com

Library of Congress Cataloging in Publication Data
Thambirajah, M. S.
Understanding school refusal : a handbook for professionals in education, health and social care / M.S. Thambirajah,
Karen J. Grandison, and Louise De-Hayes.
p. cm.
Includes bibliographical references and index.
ISBN-13: 978-1-84310-567-1 (pb : alk. paper) 1. School attendance. I. Grandison, Karen J. II. De-Hayes, Louise.
III. Title.
LC142.T53 2008
371.2'94--dc22

2007030122

British Library Cataloguing in Publication Data
A CIP catalogue record for this book is available from the British Library

ISBN 978 1 84310 567 1

Printed and bound in Great Britain by
Athenaeum Press, Gateshead, Tyne and Wear

Contents

Figures

Tables

Preface

This book grew out of the work that the authors and their colleagues have been doing (and the frustration experienced) in addressing the issue of school refusal. Over the last five years a small group of likeminded individuals from education psychology, home tuition services and child and adolescent mental health services have been meeting regularly to share their concerns and experiences in dealing with this group of children. A consistent finding was that these children were easily recognisable; they constituted a heterogeneous group; a number of professionals were 'involved', and they posed a challenge to all the professionals caught up with them. Moreover, the stories of these children were more complex than simple generalisations could capture. As the professional group shared their experiences and their frustrations in managing them as best as they could, it became obvious that no one professional or service could do justice to them and it required the concerted efforts of all agencies involved with the child.

During the discussions in the work group it became apparent that workers in the frontline, especially schools and education welfare, were not detecting school refusal (as opposed to truancy) early enough. The effect of this delay was that management of school refusal became long and drawn out and consequently the results of interventions were rather poor. One of the main reasons for this state of affairs was that school refusal went unrecognised or was misidentified. In the course of our work we realised that schools were central to the process of proper and early identification of school refusal and were pivotal in any intervention programme.

Hence the objective of this book is twofold: first, to provide the basics of school refusal (and there is a respectable volume of literature on the subject) so that frontline professionals in education, health and social care understand the issue better. Second, to highlight the issue of school refusal for, at present, it receives little attention and remains concealed somewhere in the statistics of school non-attenders. As the title of the book indicates, it is aimed at frontline professionals such as teachers, especially those entrusted with the task of monitoring attendance, special needs co-ordinators, education welfare officers, school health advisors, community workers, social care workers and those in the voluntary sector who work with school children. Professionals and workers in education psychology, pupil referral units, child and adolescent mental health services and community paediatrics will find the material in the book relevant and useful.

The authors have attempted to keep the length of the book short and its contents precise. This has been achieved by some sacrifices. It is hoped that the interested reader will peruse the references provided at the end of the book. We have also endeavoured to simplify the subject. Subject-orientated textbooks are about generalities and typical cases while practice is about particularities and individual cases. Each child with school refusal requires an individualised approach.

Lastly, the authors wish to express their thanks and gratitude to the colleagues of their respective teams and most of all to the children and parents who provided them with the experience of and material for this book.

M. S. Thambirajah
Karen J. Grandison
Louise De-Hayes

Abbreviations Used in the Book

CAMHS – child and adolescent mental health services

CBT – cognitive behaviour therapy

DfES – Department for Education and Skills

EBSR – emotionally-based school refusal

EOTAS – [suitable] education otherwise than at school

EP – educational psychologist

EWO – education welfare officer

EWS – education welfare services

GP – general practitioner

IAP – individual action plan

LEA – local education authority

OCD – obsessive compulsive disorder

PRU – pupil referral unit

RSP – return to school plan

SEN – special educational needs

SENCo – special educational needs co-ordinator

SHA – school health advisor (school nurse)

SNA – school non-attendance

SR – school refusal

SRAS – school refusal assessment scale

1 Introduction: School Non-attendance

Many children and young people do not attend school at some point in their school career, but for the vast majority of pupils this tends to be occasional and relatively infrequent. The term *school non-attendance* (SNA) or school absenteeism is used here as a broad umbrella term to capture all those pupils who fail to attend school. It is used as a descriptive term that characterises the child's behaviour – the failure to attend school. School non-attendance may be initiated by the child, parents or peers; reasonable or unreasonable; occasional or persistent; motivated by pressures at school, from family or peers and sanctioned or unsanctioned by the parents or school. In short, children fail to attend school for a multitude of reasons. It may be occasional and infrequent or persistent and long lasting. It also varies from country to country. In underdeveloped countries the commonest cause of school non-attendance is poverty.

By law, in most countries parents of children of compulsory school age (5–16) are required to ensure that their children receive a suitable education by regular attendance at school or otherwise. Failure to comply with this statutory duty can lead to prosecution. In the UK, local authorities are responsible in law for making sure that pupils attend school. School attendance figures are published annually.

Children who fail to attend school are not a uniform group and SNA, especially when it is prolonged and persistent, remains a puzzling and complex problem. Various agencies and authorities classify them into different groups depending on their agency priorities. Official guidance to schools on the different reasons for absence distinguishes between two groups:

Authorised absence: This is absence from school with permission from a teacher or other authorised representative from school. Here the school has either given approval in advance for the pupil to be absent or has accepted an explanation offered afterwards as satisfactory justification for the absence (e.g. illness in the child, bereavement in the family).

Unauthorised absence: This is absence from school without permission from a teacher or other authorised representative from school. This includes all unjustified absences such as lateness, holidays during term time not authorised by the school, absence when the reason is not yet established and, more importantly, truancy.

Where a pupil is absent, schools have a duty to register the absence as authorised or unauthorised, and are obliged to take firm action in instances of unauthorised absences. In educational circles the grouping or classification of SNA most often goes no further than the division into the above two categories. Many education authorities tend to equate unauthorised absences with truancy, perhaps driven more by administrative and strategic objectives than by reality. Nevertheless, most educational reports and studies acknowledge a subgroup within unauthorised absences: *parentally condoned absences*. These are unauthorised absences resulting from parents keeping pupils away from school. Also called parental withholding, in this subgroup parents are thought to keep the child away from school without good reason, usually for their own purposes such as looking after a sibling or to do domestic chores. From an educational point the division of persistent unauthorised absence into truancy and parentally condoned absence makes sense because the manner in which each of these form of school absence has to be managed is different.

The issue of school attendance is currently the focus of intense activity in schools and local education authorities (LEAs) in England. A number of studies have established that it is a widespread problem. The National Child Developmental Study found that one in ten school pupils in Britain was absent at any one time (Fogelman, Tibbenham and Lambert 1980). The Audit Commission (1999) estimated that at least 40,000 of the total of 400,000 pupils were absent from school each day. At the time of writing the Department for Education and Skills publishes annual figures for school non-attendance. It is also a high priority policy concern for which the government has set a target to reduce levels of non-attendance. By 2008 school absences are to be reduced by 8 per cent compared with 2005 (Department for Education and Employment 1999; DfES 2002).

The most recent figures from the DfES show that in 2005/6 pupil absence was in total 6.68 per cent of which 5.89 per cent were authorised absences and 0.7 per cent unauthorised (DfES 2006). This represents half-day sessions missed as a percentage of total possible sessions. Translated into simple figures, it means that 1.4 million children missed school during this period. These findings have led to sensational newspaper headlines such as 'one in five was out of school without permission from school' (Meikle 2006). On average, each student in primary school missed the equivalent of four days of education in the year and those in secondary schools were absent for seven days during the year. It is worth emphasising that just 1 per cent of secondary school pupils accounted for more than a third of all unauthorised absences implying that there was a core group of pupils who showed a habitual pattern of frequent absence from school.

Apart from the legal requirement, SNA is a cause for concern for a number of reasons. First, loss of schooling is associated with poor academic performance and reduced attainment. This inevitably leads to reduced life chances and poor employment opportunities. Second, school non-attenders lose out on the age appropriate socialisation and peer relationships. Third, for a significant minority, it is associated with later psychosocial difficulties and the long-term outcome is poor in persistent school non-attenders (see Appendix I).

Official statistics on school non-attendance are crude measures that hide a number of subgroups. For example, as mentioned, unauthorised absence is made of at least two groups, truants and parentally condoned absences and the figures do not tell us about the latter group. More importantly, hidden somewhere in the statistics is a small but significant subgroup of school non-attenders variously called school phobics, school refusers and school avoiders. The hallmark of this group is that they show severe emotional distress at the prospect of attending school and many, indeed, have an emotional disorder. Often they are misclassified as truants; the parents are blamed for their inability to get these children to attend school or they may masquerade as medically sanctioned absences. This category of school non-attenders has been recognised by educationalist and health professionals for more than 75 years. Yet they are ignored in official statistics and remain largely invisible. This third group, commonly known as school refusal (SR), is the subject of this book, but before discussing it further it is important to clarify the usage of the various terms that have been employed to describe the different subgroups of school non-attenders. Lack of consistency in the terminology used to describe and depict the various subgroups has been a major barrier to our understanding SNA.

Terminology

Historically a variety of terms have been used to describe the various groups of children who fail to attend school. Terms such as truancy, SR or similar terms often continue to be used without precision and sometimes interchangeably. Research commissioned by the Local Government Association (Archer, Filmer-Sankey and Fletcher-Campbell 2003) showed that there was no clear definition among practitioners in LEAs and schools distinguishing between the various groups of school refusers. The study also noted that there was lack of clarity about the definitions of the various terms used to describe this group. Only 17 per cent of the 818 schools in the study identified SR or school phobia (these terms were used interchangeably by most schools) as a separate category of non-attenders, although in the schools that recognised it as a subgroup there were 293 pupils who fitted the description.

In the following section we attempt to clarify the various terms used to describe groups of children who fail to attend school by defining their core characteristics as they are currently understood by authorities and researchers in the field. The definitions refer to typical or 'pure' cases. In reality it is more complicated and accurate identification may be difficult (discussed further below). The following list summarises the salient features of each group and Figure 1.1 provides a classification of SNA.

- *Truancy*: absence from school without the knowledge, approval or consent of parents or school authorities.

- *Parentally condoned absence*: unauthorised school absence in which the parents keep the child at home for reasons of their own.

- *School phobia*: an outdated term that was used to describe a specific fear of a school situation (such as assembly) leading to SNA.

- *Separation anxiety*: extreme difficulties in separation from the attachment figure usually leading to SR.

- *School refusal* (SR): difficulties attending school or absence from school on account of severe emotional difficulties at the time of attending school.

Truancy: The term truancy is assigned to students who absent themselves from school without permission of parents, guardian, teachers or any other person in authority; neither the parent nor school knows his or her whereabouts. Among students this is commonly known as 'wagging' and 'skiving'.

Parentally condoned absences: Sometimes called parental withholding, this refers to a situation where the parent keeps the child at home intentionally or colludes with the child in missing school. It is held that the parent approves of the absence for their own need (e.g. for company or to run errands) or is not sufficiently concerned about the loss of schooling.

School phobia: Phobia is a psychological term used to indicate irrational and extreme fear. Contemporary notion of phobias is that these are fears that are excessive to the situation and difficult to explain rationally; the object of fear is usually a real situation or event (Marks 1969). For example, the term arachnophobia is used to describe an extreme and disabling fear of spiders and creepy crawlies. School phobia means a specific fear of school or some aspect of it is eliciting the excessive fear reaction in the child. Most authorities agree that this is hardly the case with the overwhelming majority of school refusers. The school itself is almost never the object of fear. More commonly, the fear and anxiety is around issues such as leaving home and parents or interacting with peers. Although the child may have a fear of specific aspects of the school situation, such as speaking in front of the class, being bullied or changing for PE, it is now generally accepted that school refusal can result from various causes, fear of aspects of school being just one of them. The use of the term 'school phobia' is therefore misleading in that it is not only technically incorrect but it also implies that the phobic stimulus is always situated in school and therefore those dealing with the problem will be required to find the 'true' phobic source. Although the term is popular with the lay public, most authorities feel it is best discarded.

School refusal (SR): The term school refusal has been used to refer to the group of children who are reluctant to or fail to attend school for *emotional reasons*. Over the last few decades the term has gained currency in literature on the subject and replaced other terms such as school phobia and school avoidance. The term SR has the added advantage of describing the actual behaviour and distinguishing these children who *cannot* attend from those truants who *will not* attend. We use the term SR to include children who are troubled by the full range of negative emotions experienced at the time of attending school, although most often the distress is one of extreme anxiety or fear at the thought of attending school. It should be noted that SR is a *description* of certain behaviour and does not allude to any cause or causes that lead to the behaviour, not least 'within child' factors. In contemporary usage the term SR refers to reluctance to attend school or school absenteeism due to severe emotional distress, especially anxiety, about attending school irrespective of the cause. This is discussed further in the next chapter.

It is important to differentiate between SR and truancy. The child with SR is invariably a good student; the truant is a poor student. Truants openly acknowledge their dislike of schools; school refusers wish they could attend. The truant usually avoids *both* home and school, whereas the school refuser stays at home. Moreover, truants fabricate excuses to cover up their absence, the child with SR draws attention to their inability to leave home or stay in school.

Separation anxiety: This refers to unrealistic and excessive fear upon separation or anticipation of separation from major attachment figures. Here the anxiety and fear is about leaving home rather than being in school. It is *one of the reasons* for children, especially young children, refusing to attend school and is not the same as SR (see Chapter 4).

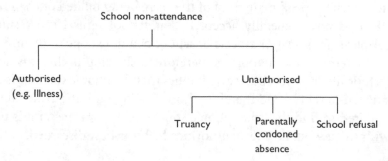

Figure 1.1 Classification of school non-attendance

Exploring school non-attendance

The first task for anyone faced with a child or young person who is reluctant to attend school or is missing school without authorisation from school is to work out to which category the SNA belongs. We suggest that this is the first necessary step towards understanding the problem and a more productive exercise than looking out for the underlying cause or causes. It is best carried out by asking four main questions (Figure 1.2).

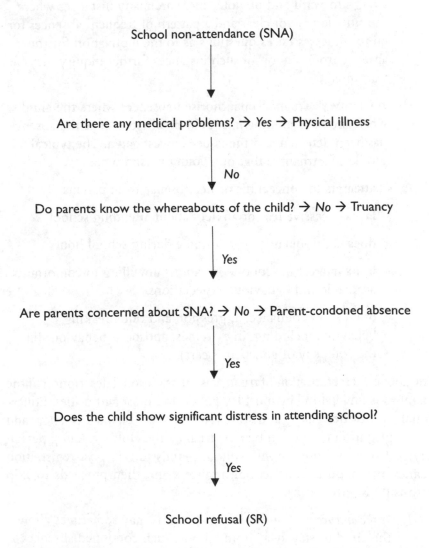

Figure 1.2 A simplified flowchart for the identification of school refusal

1. *Is there a physical illness that accounts for the non-attendance?* Physical illness in the child or young person is by far the commonest cause for a child to be away from school. These are usually authorised absences that are medically sanctioned. The illnesses may be mild and self-limiting, such as sore throats and bronchitis, or be due to hospitalisations or chronic and long-standing illnesses. While in most cases of absence due to medical reasons the basis for non-attendance is straightforward and obvious, there are many instances where the situation is not clear and a pattern of frequent absences for minor illnesses raises questions as to the motivation for the absence from school. In such instances further inquiry may be warranted.

2. *Is it truancy?* Truancy, unauthorised absences where the child's whereabouts is unknown, should be obvious once the absence has been detected and the issue is investigated. The typical profile of a truant is that of a young person who:

   ○ attempts to conceal his or her absence from parents

   ○ lacks excessive fear or anxiety about attending school

   ○ does not frequently stay at home during school hours

   ○ lacks interest in schoolwork and is unwilling to conform to academic and behaviour expectations

   ○ often shows defiance, aggression and rule breaking behaviour including, in extremes, antisocial behaviour (in the company of antisocial peers).

The above characterisation of truancy is the traditional description of the truant as is understood by most lay public and most authorities. Educational authorities make a distinction between blanket truancy and post-registration truancy. In blanket truancy the child or young person stays off one or more lessons without permission; in post-registration truancy the pupil attends school, registers and then proceeds to skip lessons (O'Keeffe 1995).

3. *Is the absence parentally condoned?* Parents may sometimes allow the child to stay away from school. Such condoned absences may be parentally motivated, as when a parent keeps the child

at home to provide support or company for them, to help with younger siblings or house chores. Other parents may not view education as a priority or be negligent. An extreme form of parentally condoned absence is when pupils are withdrawn from school by parents (e.g. following conflicts with schools or teachers). In such circumstances parents are legally obliged to demonstrate that they are providing 'out of school education' and failure to do so is regarded as parentally condoned absence.

4. *Does the child show significant emotional distress about attending school?* Presence of severe emotional distress at the time of attending school, such as excessive anxiety including physical symptoms, is the distinguishing feature of SR. In contrast to truants, SR is associated with:

   • emotional symptoms rather than behavioural ones

   • parental awareness of their absence from school

   • the child staying at home during school hours

   • the child having no emotional distress during weekends and school holidays

   • the child displaying no significant antisocial behaviours and complying with school work. The main differences between truancy and SR are summarised in Table 1.1.

Although the simplified description presented above is a useful starting point for identifying SR and has heuristic value, in some instances it may not be as straightforward as it appears. Difficulties in classifying school non-attenders into one or the other group arises mainly from two sources: uncertainty about the presentation and overlap between the various categories. Professionals working with this group of children may sometimes encounter the following ambiguous presentations:

   • *Uncertainty about the presence of physical illness.* A common dilemma faced by non-medical professionals dealing with school refusers is when the grounds for presence of a physical illness in the child are doubtful or questionable. Frequent medically sanctioned absences should alert the practitioner to the possibility of SR or parentally condoned absence. Many general practitioners (GPs) unwittingly fall into the trap of providing medical excuses for such absences. A variation of the same theme is when a small minority of children with chronic physical illnesses and disabilities take excessive amounts of time off school even after accounting for their physical condition.

• *Physical symptoms for which no cause has been found:* Some children may complain of physical symptoms for which no medical cause has been found after repeated examinations and investigations. This raises two questions:

1. Are these physical symptoms due to anxiety or other psychological issues?

2. Is the child malingering, i.e. complaining of being ill to avoid school?

The consensus is that the first group of children should be viewed as school refusers. For the second group it raises the subsidiary question of why the child is trying so hard to avoid school.

Table 1.1 Features distinguishing school refusal and truancy

School refusal	Truancy
Severe emotional distress about attending school; may include anxiety, physical symptoms or temper tantrums	Lack of excessive anxiety or fear about attending school
Parents are aware of the absence; child often tries to persuade parents to allow him or her stay at home	Child often attempts to conceal absence from school; parents are usually unaware of the child's whereabouts
Absence of significant antisocial behaviours such as aggressive behaviours and fighting	Frequently shows behaviour problems such as disruptive acts (e.g. stealing, fighting, lying), often in the company of antisocial peers
During school hours, the child stays at home because it is considered a safe and secure environment	During school hours, child usually does not stay at home
Child expresses willingness to do schoolwork and complies with completing work at home	Lacks interest in school work and is unwilling to conform to academic and behaviour expectations

- *Covert parental support for the child to stay at home.* Some parents find it difficult to withstand the relentless pressure put upon them by the school refuser and may give in to the demands. This reinforces the child's behaviour. Other parents may collude with the child for reasons of their own. In some instances parents find it unbearable to witness the extreme anxiety shown by the children and may decide to let them stay at home.

- *The truant who stays at home.* Although the stereotype of the truant is one whose parents are unaware of their absence from school, some truants stay at home with their parent's knowledge. Parents have little control over these children and feel helpless to get them into school. This is more common with adolescents and is characterised by lack of emotional distress and absence of mental health problems. Indeed they show little guilt about keeping away from school and are little interested in school work. Often they are happy at home, organising their life around themselves to the exclusion of school and may not show prominent behaviour problems as long as they are allowed to stay at home. This is a less well recognised group and their absence is usually sanctioned by the medical profession.

Reasons for under-recognition of school refusal

As mentioned above, official figures do not take SR into consideration and therefore there are no official estimates of the extent of the problem. Most teachers, especially those involved in special education, are aware of the problem, but it is not unusual for it to go unrecognised for a considerable period of time. This may be due to several reasons:

- *Lack of awareness of the extent and impact of SR:* Many educational professionals do not consider SR as an entity separate from truancy and parentally condoned absences. In the study by Archer *et al.* (2003) regarding the understanding among schools about school refusal and social phobia across 60 LEAs only 17 per cent of the schools had provision for identifying it as a separate group. The survey also found that teachers often tended to blame the parents for the child's non-attendance.

- *Difficulties in distinguishing SR from other groups of SNA*: Features of SR have to be actively investigated and this requires both knowledge of the condition and a degree of skill. Many teachers are handicapped by practical amenities like lack of time and space, where children and parents can be seen in privacy to obtain a reasonable description of the problem. Moreover, some children present with a mixed picture that makes identification difficult. For example, some school refusers show 'defensive aggression' (see Chapter 2) in that they use aggressive behaviour to prevent exposing themselves to the anxiety-provoking situation (such as separation from parents) thus masking the underlying features of SR.

- *Invisibility*: As a group, school refusers are well-behaved children. Unlike children who show difficult behaviour, school refusers are compliant and likable children and therefore do not stand out in class. They are often academically above average and may not come to the attention of teachers and hence remain an invisible group.

- *Excluding medical conditions*: Ruling out medical reasons for absence from school is sometimes not easy and teachers tend to give the benefit of doubt to the child.

- *Blaming parents*: Blaming parents for the absence of the children is easy if one does not look carefully at the case.

In general there is a tendency in society for emotional problems to remain largely unacknowledged. Whereas teachers and other school professionals are very aware of the effects of physical illnesses on schooling, the impact of emotional problems remains mostly unrecognised. This is more so in the case of children who appear 'normal' and well behaved. This is perhaps a reflection of a more general attitude of our society where physical or medical problems get recognition and sympathy while emotional or mental health problems are poorly understood and go unacknowledged.

In this introductory chapter we have looked at the 'bigger picture' of SNA to set the context for our discussion on SR so that practitioners can position themselves to better understand it. In the next chapter we examine the features of SR in greater detail.

The case of Ben

Ben, a 12-year-old boy, came to the attention of his form teacher, Mrs Leahy, when she noticed that his school attendance was getting poor. In the latter part of the third term he had missed two or more days each week. She started paying more attention when she observed that one morning he had refused to get out of his mother's car. Mrs Leahy had coaxed him to come into school. But he had complained of stomach ache and diarrhoea. She had got him to sit in the school nurse's clinic room and asked him to take his time till his stomach settled down. He had been visibly distressed, agitated and shaky, but he could not tell her what the problem was or what was bothering him. After spending about half an hour in the clinic room he had requested to go back into class. Mrs Leahy was surprised to see him recover so quickly and join the rest of the class. There had been no problems for the rest of the day.

Ben had moved from the primary school at the beginning of September the previous year. At primary school he had been a polite, well-behaved boy; he had a good group of friends. He was academically able and was in the top set for most of the subjects. He was particularly good at maths. Going through his attendance record Mrs Leahy discovered that his attendance had been almost 100 per cent in the first term in secondary school but had declined during the second term, with a few days off, and the absences were now becoming more frequent. Most absences had been supported by medical certificates.

Mrs Leahy had been struck by the high level of distress he had shown when getting out of the car, and was even more surprised by the way he had bounced back after spending a brief period of time in the clinic room. As far as she knew, he came from a 'normal' family and there was no indication that he was being bullied at school. She wondered what was going on.

In the subsequent chapters we will be following up Ben's story as it unravels.

Summary points

- SNA or pupil absenteeism is common; while most absences are authorised by school authorities, in about one out of five pupils the absence is unauthorised.

- The main reasons for authorised school absence are illnesses and family events (e.g. bereavements). Unauthorised absences may be due to parentally condoned absences, truancy or SR. Overlap between the three categories is not uncommon.

- Truancy and SR are distinct entities and show very different features and correlates (see Table 1.1).

- School refusal (formerly also called school phobia) is defined as school non-attendance (or extreme reluctance to attend school) due to significant emotional distress at the prospect of attending school.

- Government and departmental directives have chiefly focused on truancy and parentally condoned absences.

- Despite the availability of voluminous research literature on the subject and the distress and disability it causes in children and families, SR remains largely a hidden problem, under-recognised and under-managed.

2 Identifying and Understanding School Refusal

> The child is absent from school for varying periods from several months to a year. The absence is consistent. At all times the parents know where the child is. It is near his mother or near home. The reason for the truancy [sic] is incomprehensible to the parents and school. The child may say that it is afraid to go to school, afraid of the teacher or say it does not know why it will not go to school. (Broadwin 1932, p.254)

The excerpt above is from Broadwin's first description of SR in 1932. He was the first to delineate it from typical truancy (although he called it a form of truancy), and was the first to record the difference between the two groups. He and other early workers noted that this group of children differed from other truants in that they were well behaved, academically average, if not above average, free of antisocial behaviour and they even liked school. Over the 75 years since the first description by Broadwin a large body of literature has accumulated that provides us with a better understanding of the profile of these children and distinguish them from truants. Table 1.1 in Chapter 1 summarises the differences between truancy and SR.

In SR, the onset of the problem may be sudden or gradual. In many instances the reluctance to attend school follows a period of legitimate absence from school, such as minor illness or school holidays. In such instances it may be viewed as an exaggeration of the ordinary unwillingness of children to attend school after a period of absence (think of adults who do not want to return to work after holidays!). In others the onset is gradual, and over a period of time the child is absent from school sporadically with a few days missed here and there. Soon a pattern of non-attendance may emerge in which the child fails to attend two to three days a week, especially missing days on which he or she has certain disliked subjects (and teachers). Many children may continue to attend in an erratic way, but at some point in its course the SR becomes continuous, resulting in prolonged absence of many weeks and months. The following description by Hersov (1977) provides a graphic picture of SR:

> The problem often starts with vague complaints of school or reluctance to attend progressing to total refusal to go to school or remain in school in the face of persuasion, entreaty, recrimination and punishment by parents and pressures from teachers, doctors and education welfare officers. The behaviour may be accompanied by overt signs of anxiety or even panic when the time comes to go to school and most children cannot even leave home to set out for school. Many who do return home half way there, and some children, once at school, rush home in a state of anxiety. Many children insist that they want to go to school and are prepared to do so but cannot manage when the time comes.

In some children the first sign of onset of school refusal is requests to leave the classroom or school, usually on the pretext of not feeling well.

Features of school refusal

Although case studies and descriptions such as the above portray a vivid picture of SR and provide us with a psychological profile of these children, research into SR has been hindered for a long time by the lack of consistency among research studies in defining this group. This was partially overcome by Berg, Nichols and Prichard (1969) when they started using explicit criteria for defining SR. Their operational definition of SR was as follows:

1. severe difficulty in attending school, often amounting to prolonged absence

2. severe emotional upset – shown by symptoms such as excessive fearfulness, undue tempers, misery or complaints of feeling ill without obvious organic cause on being faced with the prospect of going to school

3. staying at home with the knowledge of the parents when they should be at school

4. absence of significant antisocial disorders such as stealing, lying, wandering, destructiveness and sexual misbehaviour.

Most of the recent research has used the above criteria or slight variations of it. A close reading of the above operational definition reveals that essentially SR consists essentially of two main components, each with varying degrees of severity:

1. an emotional component consisting of emotional distress at the time attending school

2. a behavioural component manifesting as SNA.

Severe emotional distress at the time of attending school

The hallmark of SR is the severe emotional distress and misery experienced by the child at the time of attending school. Typically the child shows no difficulties until the time comes to get ready in the morning to go to school. At the time of going to school the child exhibits severe emotional distress often accompanied by physical symptoms such as nausea, vomiting, shaking, sweating, diarrhoea or difficulties in breathing. This is accompanied by refusal to get ready, leave home or get into the car. When persuaded to be taken to school many children refuse to get out of the car and fight the parent's efforts. Others go into a state of panic once at school and may want their parents to take them home. Yet others may have difficulties remaining in lessons and may want to leave.

Often the child and the parents are unable to identify the emotions that underpin the reluctance of the child to attend school. Many children describe it as a dread or unknown fear. For example, one 12-year-old boy described the feeling 'as if something terrible was going to happen but did not know what'. A 13-year-old girl described the feeling as follows: 'something overcomes you; you become a different person; it is as if it is the end of the world for you'. Frequently the child lacks the vocabulary to describe the experience, apart from saying that they feel scared. Often they need help to put their experience into words but the adult needs to be careful about 'putting words into the child's mouth'. The difficulties the children have in articulating their subjective emotional state and the difficulties parents and teachers have in understanding the children's experience is the commonest reason for the under-recognition of SR. Parents and teachers may feel the child is 'putting it on' or deceiving them in order to stay in the comfort of the home. Teachers often think that the parents are not assertive enough or are colluding with the child.

The degree of emotional distress exhibited by the children varies enormously. Some are physically sick and paralysed with fear, while others partially manage to cope with the distress and attend school. A prominent feature of the emotional distress shown by the child is that once the decision not to go to school has been made the child shows a remarkable recovery and is back to his usual self. This instant return to normality is one that the parents and teachers find hard to understand. In the vast majority of instances what one witnesses is a child showing a high degree of anxiety that rapidly dissipates once the perceived threat abates or is removed. The same is true of weekends and school holidays. During these periods the child is remarkably well and healthy. A good grasp of the features of anxiety and its nature is crucial to understanding school refusal. Chapter 3 describes anxiety and its manifestations.

School attendance difficulties

These include a whole range of difficulties from full school attendance to outright unwillingness and refusal, resulting in a pattern of total non-attendance for varying periods of time. SR is best conceptualised as a continuum with various degrees of severity. Many children continue to attend with great difficulty and although the parents may be aware of the problems teachers may not. Their attendance may be 100 per cent, but this may be achieved at a cost. Such children show extreme reluctance to go to school as well as high levels of anxiety at the prospect of attending, yet manage to get to school (with great difficulty either) because the parents prevail on them or because the child may be just managing to cope with the anxiety on their own. A little exploration of their mental state may reveal prominent anxiety symptoms, although the child, parent or teachers may be unable to identify them precisely. Others manage to attend school for most days but their attendance record may show occasional school absence or avoidance of certain days or lessons. In others there are periods of sporadic absences that last a few days and commonly a pattern of absence is evident. For example, one 12-year-old boy said, 'It is Mondays and Tuesdays that I can't manage. Other days are alright and Friday is the best day; we have IT on Fridays and I like it.'

In some instances school avoidance is clouded by the presence of frequent minor ailments that may or may not be medically sanctioned. Commonly, various medical excuses ranging from frequent minor infections to recurrent physical problems may be given as excuses for the absence and it is not unusual, in such instances, for parents to find it difficult to see through the assumption of the sick role by the child; other parents may give the benefit of the doubt to the child and thus implicitly collude with them. In a significant minority of children the SNA becomes persistent with appreciable absence. It may take the form of sporadic absence with loss of school days here and there, or be continuous and last for weeks and months.

In some children the difficulties manifest as minor forms of SR and often the first sign may be frequent requests to leave the classroom on the pretext of wanting to go to the toilet. Others may frequently complain of not feeling well and wanting to be excused from class or school. Typically these complaints are about feeling sick or 'feeling ill'. Teachers may find a safe place for the child to spend time, such as the library or the nurse's room. The child may want to speak to the parents by phone and prevail on them to pick them up.

The varying degrees of SR are illustrated in Figure 2.1. Those with less severe SR are usually managed by educational staff while those who show severe degree of difficulties are referred to other services such as the child and adolescent mental health services.

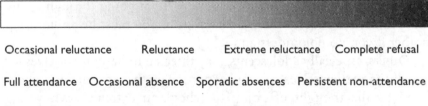

| Occasional reluctance | Reluctance | Extreme reluctance | Complete refusal |

| Full attendance | Occasional absence | Sporadic absences | Persistent non-attendance |

Figure 2.1 The spectrum of school refusal ranging from occasional reluctance to attend school to complete school refusal resulting in persistent non-attendance

Apart from the emotional distress and SNA two other constellations of behaviours that may be seen in school refusal are worthy of note, for these aspects of the presentation often leads to confusion and misidentification of the problem. These include:

1. behaviours that are used to avoid the mental anguish

2. secondary complications arising from SR.

Other avoidance behaviours

The prime aim of the school refuser is to avoid experiencing anxiety and the dread that accompanies it by evading the situation that provokes his or her anxiety. They find the anxiety resulting from the thought of attending school overwhelming and escaping the anxiety-provoking situation resolves the problem, albeit temporarily. Apart from frank refusal to attend, these avoidance behaviours take several forms. One course of action left to the child is to fight back. This manifests as 'defensive aggression' and may manifest as temper tantrums, aggressive outbursts and, in some cases, a show of violence at the prospect of attending school. Some become uncharacteristically abusive and rude to the person trying to get him or her into school. Use of aggression to avoid school may be mistaken for wilful avoidance of school. But the child is otherwise well behaved and often regrets his or her actions. Clinging on to one parent in the hope of being rescued by that parent is another ruse used by some children. Making the parent feel guilty for attempting to coax them into going to school is a common form of emotional blackmail employed by younger children. One seven-year-old girl yelled at her mother, 'You are horrible. You don't love me. I hate you.' The mother was taken aback by the ferocity with which the words were said and burst into tears. The implied message was, 'I am going through agony and you do not understand my mental pain. You must be an uncaring mother if you do not understand it.'

Others, especially adolescents, may threaten to harm themselves (or actually harm themselves) to avoid experiencing the high anxiety engendered by the thought of going to school. In extreme cases young children may threaten to jump out of the window or threaten to run away from home. Although deliberate self-harm is rare in this group, some children may indulge in token attempts to harm themselves by superficially cutting themselves or wandering away from home. Although such behaviours are confusing and sometimes alarming, they are best understood as a part of avoidance behaviours, the aim of which is to cope with anxiety. The role of avoidance behaviours in anxiety is discussed in Chapter 3.

Complications and secondary handicaps

One of the adverse outcomes of SR is that once it has begun a vicious cycle of increasing anxiety and escalating school avoidance gets established very rapidly. As school and other professionals try to identify and make sense of the school absence, valuable time is lost and the problems get entrenched and more difficult to overcome. Prolonged school absence creates complications of its own.

- The child falls behind in school work which makes return to school more difficult because it may reinforce the fear of failure the child already has.

- The loss of routine and getting used to spending time at home, including indulgence in pleasurable activities such as daytime television, computer games or accessing the internet provide positive reinforcement of non-attendance.

- The loss of friends and peer contact leads to social isolation. Meanwhile their friends find new friends of their own and move on. Many persistent school refusing children become fearful of meeting peers or bumping into them and dare not venture out. Many such children claim that they are alright with young people whom they do not know, for example, on holidays but are terrified of meeting their classmates.

- Anxiety worsens due to avoidance of the feared situation. Although avoiding school reduces anxiety for that day, the net result is to increase it the next day when it comes to attending school. In due course anxiety becomes entrenched and the child becomes more fearful of attending school. Moreover, over time, generalisation of anxiety to other situations occurs and it is not uncommon for the child to be anxious in non-school situations such as travelling by bus, going to the local shop and going out with family. Any prospect of meeting people, especially young people, becomes a nightmare and soon the child may become housebound. As result the child becomes isolated, loses the little self-confidence he or she had had in the past and feels depressed, leading to crippling secondary social and personal disability. The vicious cycle of events is shown in Figure 2.2.

The following account by a school nurse who visited a 15-year-old girl called Alice who had not been able to attend school for more than two school terms illustrates the devastating effect of prolonged SR:

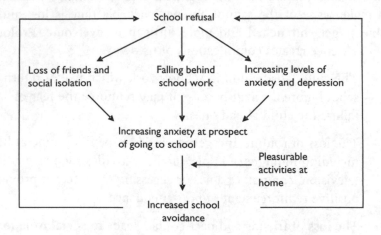

Figure 2.2 The vicious cycle in school refusal

Alice

On my arrival Alice ran upstairs and sat against the bedroom door so that no one could enter. She had told her mother that she had no problems and did not want to speak to anyone. She refused to come down and I had to speak to her through the door. Alice's replies were very brief, sometimes one-worded and sometimes there was silence. When Alice went back to school at the beginning of the school year she was moved from Group 2 where she had been on top to Group 1. She was worried about PE and complained of headaches. Arrangements were made for her to be excused from taking part in PE. Things became worse when the school arranged a trip to London. She became increasingly worried about going and was worried about what would happen if she got lost or a bomb went off. Two weeks prior to the end of the term she rang her mother from school asking to come home early. Then she stopped going to school altogether. This was five months ago.

Now Alice spends her entire day at home. She will not get dressed till 2.00 p.m. She gets up from bed about 10.00 a.m. and goes to bed after midnight and spends long periods of time on internet chat lines. The only work she does at home is to wash the laundry and put it to dry on the line, she will not do any other work. She will play football in the back garden with her 12-year-old brother and some children from the neighbourhood who are five to seven years of age. She does the minutes and reports for her mother who is the secretary for the local football team and organises the subscriptions. Although she is comfortable and relaxed at home she will not answer the door or take telephone calls. She does not keep in touch with her friend by phone or email. When one of her friends called in to see her, she refused to go out with her and was not keen on seeing her again. She has a number of pets: three fish, eight rabbits, two cats and one dog, all of which she cares for very well. Her mother had wanted to seek help from the GP but Alice will not go to the GP and when the GP made a home visit she had locked herself in the room and refused to see him.

Hopefully, most children will come to the attention of educational and other professionals early in the course and receive the necessary help to overcome the problem. Nevertheless it should be noted that SR has the potential to lead to long-term disability (see Appendix I, Prognosis).

It is worth pointing out that *any* child or young person who had been away from school and been confined to the house (e.g. following prolonged illness) would be experiencing most of the secondary effects of SNA mentioned above and distinguishing between the initial picture of SR and the secondary handicaps resulting from them can be difficult.

Factors contributing to school refusal

It is important to emphasise that SR is not only about the child but also about the school, as well as the parents. Examination of the literature reveals that SR (and most other problems in children) is multiply determined by factors that are operating at various levels of ecology. Thus, it is impossible to uncover a single factor or a single pathway that ultimately leads to SR. The search for the one factor (the 'main effect') responsible for SR is insufficient to explain the problem. Rather the literature confirms that SR occurs when stress exceeds support, when risks are greater than resilience and when 'pull' factors that promote SNA overcome the 'push' factors that encourage attendance. It is usually a unique combination of various factors and their interaction that leads to SNA, although one factor may be more salient to the problems than others in a particular child.

A useful framework for thinking about the various elements that ultimately lead to SR is to consider the various factors in the child, family and school separately. However, reference to 'factors' that contribute to SR should not lead one to view the problem in an oversimplified fashion. These factors are not independent of one another, nor are they static and unchanging. Another important issue is the direction of causality. Does poor peer relationship lead to SR or does SR lead to reduced opportunities for developing of peer relationships? In short, what one considers to be the cause of the problem may turn out to be its consequence. Current evidence points towards the fact that factors from these three domains interact with one another in a reciprocal and interactive fashion. For example, a child with specific reading learning difficulties (child factor) may not have been identified by school (school factor) and be receiving excessive help at home (over-involvement of parents).

Child factors

The typical profile of the school refuser may be described as follows: they tend to be introverted and have low self-confidence and low self-esteem. They easily get overwhelmed by stress and tend to be anxious and fearful. Often they are more dependent and immature; they may be socially isolated and experience difficulties in peer relationships. Many, but not all, find separation from the mother difficult from an early age. Their poor self-concept renders them sensitive to criticism, let alone bullying. Although they are as good as or even better than other children in terms of intelligence and academic performance they do not think much of themselves and are self-critical and emotionally fragile. Parents often say that during their infancy and toddlerhood they were inhibited, clingy and not venturesome. This constellation of traits in infancy has been termed *behavioural inhibition*. It refers to a temperamental style characterised by reluctance to interact and withdrawal from unfamiliar settings, people or objects. In infants this manifests as irritability, in toddlers as shyness and fearfulness and in school-age children as cautiousness, reticence and introversion. Additionally, learning difficulties, general or specific, known or unknown, subtle or obvious may render the child unwilling to attend school. Fear of failure and social sensitivity is a feature of many school refusers. Other developmental problems such as autism spectrum disorders are sometimes a contributory factor, especially when the problems are subtle and remain unidentified.

Family factors

Family transitions like parental separation and divorce or birth of a sibling may contribute significantly to SR. Loss and bereavements, family social and financial stress may play a part in the problem and should not be underestimated. Physical and mental health problems in parents are another source of stress for the child. Apart from family stress, certain dysfunctional family patterns have been described in the literature on the subject. Before describing 'family dysfunction' associated with school refusing children, it must be emphasised that there is no such thing as a 'normal' family; every family has its own strengths and weakness and descriptions of these often depend on who is describing them. Yet there is evidence that certain family factors are more commonly seen in children with anxiety and separation problems including SR. These include parental overprotection, anxiety disorders in parents and high levels of family stress. The stereotypic description of a family with a child who experiences separation difficulties and SR is a triangular relationship between an overprotective mother, a distant father and an over-dependent child. This may be true of some families but certainly not the case in a majority.

School factors

The most common school factor that contributes to SR is peer bullying at school. The most destructive aspect of bullying is that it damages the child's sense of developing self. Bullying takes various forms and may be verbal or physical. Most children who are bullied suffer in secret and are reluctant to talk about it. A third form of bullying, termed relational bullying, is equally damaging to children. It is defined as the purposeful damage and manipulation of peer relationships leading to social exclusion (Crick and Grotpeter 1992). It includes ignoring, isolating, excluding and shunning. Other common peer problems take the form of difficulties in social interaction and in making and keeping friends. Difficulties in coping with academic demands either due to undetected learning difficulties or problems with certain subjects are common reasons for dissatisfaction with the school. PE is often cited by pupils as a cause of difficulties.

By far the most benign cause of SR is transition to senior school. A significant minority of pupils at the end of their first year at the secondary school show 'cross-phase dip'. This is a dip in performance and motivation brought about by the move from one school to another and occurs especially in Year 7 pupils. Some find the move to the 'big school' hard to manage. One boy explained the transition difficulties as: 'The school is huge and we have to go from classroom to classroom and everybody seemed tall. The teachers are busy and have no time for us.' One

11-year-old boy described his vulnerability as follows: 'I am the shortest in class, other boys look like giants. They are so rough and loud. I feel I'll get trampled.'

The factors that precipitate SR may be different from those that perpetuate the behaviour. For example, reluctance to attend school after a period of absence due to hospitalisation or a minor illness in the child may be handled by parents by giving into the demands of the child, perhaps due to anxieties of their own about the safety of the child in school, thereby maintaining his SR. Other systemic factors associated with SR include school size, frequent change of school staff, and structure of the school day including transition times between lessons. The various factors that may contribute to the onset and maintenance of SR are given in Table 2.1, and Figure 2.3 provides a framework for understanding how these factors may lead to SR.

Understanding the interaction between environmental factors, the family and the child is necessary to promote proper understanding of the nature of SR and generate strategies for its effective management and prevention.

Table 2.1 Common factors contributing to school refusal

School factors	Child factors	Family factors
Bullying	Separation difficulties	Recent family transitions
Transition to secondary school or change of school	Anxieties regarding interacting with peers	Recent losses in the family
Unidentified general or specific learning difficulties	Fear of failure, poor self-confidence	Significant changes in the family
Poor Special Educational Needs (SEN) provision	Other developmental problems	Anxiety or other mental health problems in parent(s)
Difficulties in specific academic subjects	Worries about parents' wellbeing	Under-involvement of father
Problems with peers at school	Fear of parental separation or that a parent will leave	Parents easily stressed by child's anxiety or protests
Activities that the child cannot manage (e.g. PE, performing in public)	Over-dependence on parents	Parental over-involvement or overprotection

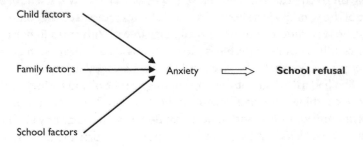

Figure 2.3 A simplified framework for understanding the various factors contributing to school refusal. Please note that the contribution of the various factors to the problem is never independent of one another as represented here, nor is the direction of causality unidirectional. The relationships are invariably reciprocal and interactional (see also Chapter 5).

The case of Ben, continued

Mrs Leahy, Ben's teacher, was curious to know Ben's attendance record. On going through the attendance register, she noticed that had been absent from school over the past two terms on a number of occasions, usually supported by a medical certificate from his general practitioner. At the beginning of the first term Ben's attendance had been 90 per cent, but in the second term he had only attained 65 per cent attendance. She wondered how this had gone unnoticed. There also seemed to be a pattern to his non-attendance. He had missed mostly Mondays and Tuesdays and, sometimes, Wednesdays. But over the term there was a distinct decline in his attendance.

Next, Mrs Leahy arranged to meet his parents. As it happened, only Ben's mother, Mrs Taylor, turned up. She was profoundly apologetic for her husband's absence. He was working and could not take time off. Ben's mother was as concerned as the teacher about Ben's attendance record. Ben, she said, lost sleep at nights worrying about attending school. In the mornings, he was restless, agitated and in and out of the bathroom several times before he got ready to school. He complained of abdominal cramps and was visibly in pain. He usually felt sick and refused to have his breakfast. As the time to leave for school approached, he would beg her to let him stay just for that day. She had great difficulty persuading him to get into the car. When they arrived at the school gates, getting him out of the car was an ordeal. He would cling on to the car seat and refuse to get out or throw his school bag out of the window in a show of temper. She was surprised that on some days he was rude to her and called her names. With tears in her eyes she said, 'It is not like him. He is a loving boy and had never been defiant or anything like that, we have not brought him up that way.'

She had asked him about any bullying at school and he had denied any such thing. She had asked his best friend Tom about possible bullying and was surprised to hear that Ben was a popular boy in school and was well liked by the class. He liked school work and always does his homework and was keen to please his teacher. Mrs Taylor said that he had experienced difficulties separating from her when he started at the primary school and it took him a long time to 'get used to it'. Thereafter he had been fine. Moving to the new school had been an ordeal for Ben and Mrs Taylor was quite sure his stomach pains and diarrhoea started when he joined the secondary school. She had taken him to the doctor several times and seen a paediatrician but they found no particular physical cause for the abdominal pains. She said that Ben had 'sensitive bowels' and added that she too was like him and suffered with irritable bowel.

Ben was the only child in the family. His father worked at building sites for a construction company and had to travel a lot. The company had been making redundancies and his job had been under threat and he had to work hard to prove himself. He had been aware of the difficulties she was experiencing in the mornings getting Ben to school. Asked what he thought about it, Mrs Taylor said that her husband was a 'no nonsense man' and felt that she was too weak and gave in to Ben easily. She added, 'he is not there in the mornings, so how will he know?'

In describing the main features of SR we have referred to emotional distress as one of the characteristic features that distinguishes it from other forms of SNA. We have also alluded to the fact that this emotional distress usually takes the form of extreme anxiety. In order to understand, identify and address SR, it is essential to have an understanding of the emotional state called anxiety – what it is, its nature and its manifestations. This is discussed in the next chapter.

Summary points

- The striking feature of SR is the presence of severe emotional distress, usually in the form of disabling anxiety, at the prospect of attending school.

- The severity of anxiety symptoms and the associated difficulties in school attendance vary from mild to very severe, ranging from occasional absence to persistent non-attendance lasting weeks, if not months.

- If undetected and untreated SR can result in social isolation, increasing anxiety, depression and severe social disability.

- As with most problems associated with children, a variety of child, family and school factors contribute to the SR; in a given child, typically a unique combination of factors of the three domains are responsible for the causation and maintenance of SR.

- Typically the children are anxious, have low self-esteem or find separation from parents difficult. The most common school factors are bulling by peers, transition or change of schools, unidentified learning difficulties and poor SEN provision. The main family factors are those associated with family transitions, bereavements and parental overprotection.

3 The Nature of Anxiety

A man questioned by the police starts to tremble and stutter; a young woman at her first job interview goes pale, asks for a glass of water and has to leave before the interview is over; a young man after meeting with an accident is 'shattered' and is unable to sleep for days; a five-year-old child starting at primary school clings on to the mother and has to be torn off her for the first few days. These are all examples of everyday anxiety. Everybody experiences it when faced with a stressful situation, as illustrated by the examples above. Anxiety is a normal and, indeed, a healthy reaction. It is normal to feel anxious when facing something difficult or dangerous and mild anxiety can be a positive and useful experience. It enables us to deal with threat or danger.

However, anxiety can become a problem if it is excessive, out of proportion to the demands of the situation or is triggered by everyday non-threatening events such as going to school. Anxiety is a feeling of uneasiness and apprehension of impending danger – even when no real threat exists. It is the tense anticipation of a threatening but vague event; a feeling of apprehension and uneasy suspense. It is closely associated with fear but not identical to it. While in the case of fear the object of fear is readily identifiable, in anxiety the threat is of the unknown and unspecific. Yet the feeling of dread and impending doom is real and existential. It is often accompanied by physical sensations such as palpitations, chest pain, shortness of breath and sweating. The state of unease and tension prompt the person to take some action to seek relief. This usually takes the form of 'fight or flight'. The 'fight or flight response' is our body's primitive, automatic, inborn response that prepares the body to 'fight' or 'flee' from perceived attack, harm or threat to our survival. In anxiety it is the 'flee' response, i.e. avoidance of the feared situation, which is most prominent.

While normal anxiety and fear serve a useful purpose in preparing oneself to face up to stressful situations and hence enhance performance (e.g. sitting for an examination) and keeping oneself safe, excessive anxiety, however, is often associated with a number of difficulties and in the extreme can cause suffering and disability. Anxiety is considered abnormal when it is prolonged, severe and when it interferes with everyday activities. In the above examples, if the young man accosted by the police continues to be incoherent for days; the young woman at the interview avoids going for future interviews; the man who had met with the accident continues to be so anxious and jumpy that he cannot get into a car and the separation difficulties in the young child persist for months so that they are unable to attend school, then one may conclude that the anxiety is disproportionate, disabling and abnormal. Since most instances of SR are anxiety-based it is important to have an understanding of what constitutes anxiety (both normal and abnormal), its nature and its characteristics.

Features of anxiety

Anyone who has been through a highly anxious or uneasy experience such as a stressful interview, losing one's way in the dark or misplacing the car keys when one is already late for work will remember what it was like to be anxious. Describing the anxiety and its various manifestations is difficult, because although it is a common experience the feelings associated with it are vague and difficult to put into words. This is significant because children who experience anxiety find it even more difficult to know what it is, let alone describe it; many young children may not have the vocabulary to describe it.

In essence, the main features of anxiety can be grouped under four headings: emotional, cognitive, physical and behavioural (Table 3.1).

Emotional features

The essential feature of anxiety is a subjective feeling of dread, apprehension and a sense of impending danger. Some describe it is as extreme nervousness, tenseness, inner restlessness and feeling on the edge. The person is convinced of the near certainty that something terrible is going to happen but is often unsure of what the impending danger is. 'I keep

Table 3.1 The core features of anxiety

Psychological	Physical	Emotional
Feeling of dread, impending doom, worry, nervousness	Dizziness, dry mouth, feeling hot, shaking	Restlessness, agitation, tense vigilance
Near certainty of harm	Sweating, palpitations	Avoidance, postponing
Expectation of danger and hypervigilance	'Butterflies in the stomach', abdominal cramps, diarrhoea	'Defensive aggression'
Thoughts of imminent catastrophe	Feeling sick, hyperventilation	Threats of self-harm

expecting something terrible is going to happen, but I don't know what it will be,' is a common complaint. The subjective feeing of distress is often so high that they may say, 'I am going to die/collapse.' Children's descriptions of anxiety states depend on their level of development. Young children often pick up on the words used by their parents; older children may describe it as scary feeling or fear. At the same time he or she is aware of the heightened state of tension and feels confused, insecure and bewildered. Often the child is consciously unaware of the source of fear or feeling of dread and may be unable to say what exactly at school causes the fear. Attempts to reassure children that things are not as terrible as they envision do not work. Other children may create unconvincing rationalisations for their fear ('the teacher is too strict', 'the toilet smells') and the worker may have to look beyond the reasons given by the child.

Physical or physiological changes

The physical manifestations of anxiety are the most noticeable. This includes all the bodily sensations that might be experienced if, for example, one has just escaped being knocked down by a car. The following symptoms can occur as a result: abdominal pains, vomiting, diarrhoea, dry mouth, sweating, rapid heartbeat (palpitation), shortness of breath, dizziness and frequent urination. Figure 3.1 shows the common bodily changes observed in anxiety. In extreme instances the person may experience panic attacks (see below).

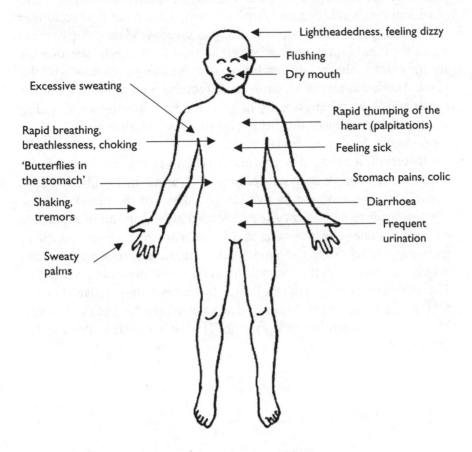

Figure 3.1 Some physical manifestations of anxiety

Behavioural features

The anxious person is restless and agitated. He or she is in a heightened state of arousal and is on the look out for dangers (hypervigilance). But the most important behavioural characteristic of anxiety is avoidance, the tendency to seek safety by evading the situation that is thought to be the cause of the perceived threat. In most cases it takes the form of avoidance of the feared situation or object. Take the case of a man who had met with a nasty accident on the way to work. The next time he has to pass the place where the accident occurred, he is bound to feel anxious and distressed. He may decide that he cannot cope with the high levels of anxiety and may avoid the place and take an alternative route to work. No doubt this would reduce his anxiety temporarily, but if he continues to avoid the place, over some time this pattern of avoidance may become established and he may never be able to pass the place in question. In short, avoidance has reinforced his anxiety about any encounter with the place. Another common scenario is of someone who faints in the town centre and feels embarrassed by it; he or she subsequently avoids going out to the town centre altogether and this may develop into disabling agoraphobia (fear of open places).

In technical terms this process is called *negative reinforcement*, the reduction of an unpleasant state of mind increasing the likelihood of the behaviour being repeated (in this case avoidance of the place). Eventually this leads to a vicious cycle of events that leads to more avoidance and more anxiety. In the case of SR, not attending school produces temporary relief from the anxiety that negatively reinforces school avoidance. Herein lies the rationale for early interventions to manage SR. The self-perpetuating nature of anxiety makes it imperative that the problem be identified and managed as soon as possible before the cycle of avoidance and reinforcement sets in. The anxiety cycle is illustrated in Figure 3.2.

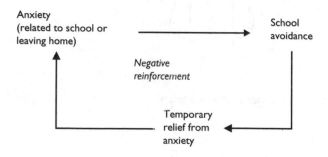

Figure 3.2 The anxiety cycle in school refusal (negative reinforcement)

Avoidance takes many forms. In order to achieve the objective of evading the anxiety provoking situation, the child may plead, beg and cajole the parent to let them stay at home. Many school refusers employ delaying tactics and take inordinately long periods of time to get ready in the morning. Others may feign illness in the hope that they may be allowed to stay at home. This may create a situation in which the parent is unsure as to whether the child is ill or not. When all strategies fail the child may become irate, angry and aggressive. They may have temper tantrums, be rude to the parent or even become violent. This 'defensive aggression' can come as a surprise to parents and teachers when a previously well-behaved child acts out of character and starts to act out. The crying, irritability and angry outbursts may be understood as disobedience, when, in fact, they represent the child's expression of fear or effort to avoid the anxiety-provoking situation. Occasionally, some children threaten self-harm or even actually harm themselves in order to avoid school. These behaviours have to be understood in the overall context of the anxiety-avoidance cycle so that interventions can be designed to get the child to overcome the difficulties.

The course of anxiety: habituation and sensitisation

Everyday anxiety is usually short lived and self-limiting. On encounter with the stressful situation anxiety levels rise rapidly but soon wane and decline quickly. In normal life most people find that in an anxiety-provoking situation such as employment interview, anxiety levels tail off after the initial ten minutes or so. Parachute jumpers' report that on jumping their anxiety rapidly reaches a peak in the first few minutes and diminishes rapidly thereafter, so much so that they even enjoy the last part of the fall! This inverted U-shaped relationship between anxiety and time in the case of 'normal' anxiety is shown in Figure 3.3a. The initial rise in arousal and anxiety levels is thought to enhance performance.

In instances of *severe* anxiety states as in SR (and in anxiety disorders), the course of anxiety tends to be somewhat different. Initially there is a very rapid rise in anxiety levels in the first few minutes resulting in extreme emotional distress and apprehension. Unable to cope with the feelings of dread and panic, at this stage the child indulges in the avoidance behaviours described above and if they are successful and as the threat of school attendance diminishes, anxiety levels return to the basal level rather quickly.

However, should the person or child withstand the exposure over a period of time without giving up, the levels of anxiety reach a plateau and surprisingly then dissipates rather rapidly. Experiments show that in most instances even in severe anxiety states the level of anxiety to return to basal levels in about half an hour and nothing untoward happens during this period. This relationship between anxiety and duration of exposure to the anxiety-provoking situation is illustrated in Figure 3.3b. This process of 'getting used to' anxiety is known as *habituation*. It is akin

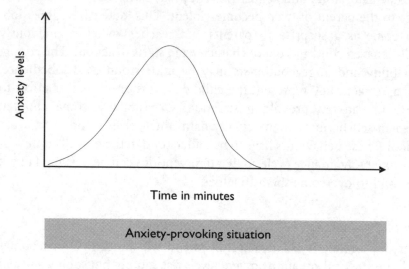

Figure 3.3a Everyday anxiety: exposure to the anxiety-provoking situation results initially in increased anxiety levels and is soon followed by rapid decline

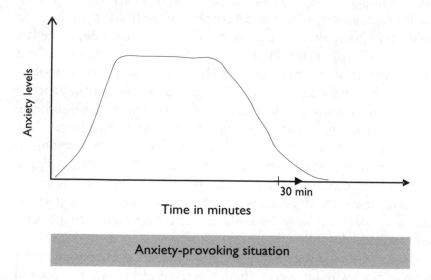

Figure 3.3b Severe anxiety: exposure to the perceived threatening situation results in an initial rapid rise in anxiety levels until it reaches a plateau and if exposure is maintained over a period of about 30 minutes or so it then returns to basal levels (habituation)

to how one adapts to the temperature of the water in the swimming pool: initially the water feels cold but after a time one gets adjusted to it. Note that it is important that for habituation to occur the person must face the stressful situation and not avoid it overtly or covertly. The essential psychological principle that underpins the management of SR (known as desensitisation) is based on the concept of habituation (see Chapter 5).

On the other hand, should one give up when anxiety levels start to rise and stage an immediate exit from the situation, the result is usually the opposite: an even steeper rise in anxiety levels on subsequent exposures. The rapid amplification of anxiety resulting from previous incomplete or partial exposure is known as *sensitisation*. The escalating anxiety levels seen in many instances of ill-planned and half-hearted attempts to get the child back to school is due to the phenomenon of sensitisation. The phenomenon of sensitisation is illustrated in Figure 3.3c.

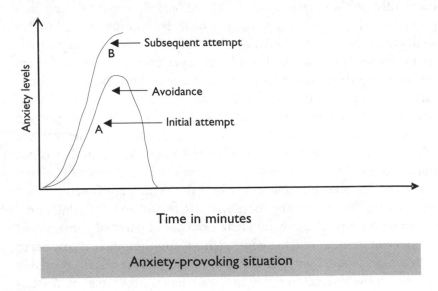

Figure 3.3c Sensitisation: In attempt A the subject has given up during the exposure situation; this produces a rapid decline in anxiety levels. But on subsequent attempt B anxiety response becomes exaggerated (sensitisation)

Coping with anxiety
Anxiety is a part of everyday life and most children and adults cope with it reasonably well. A certain amount of anxiety is helpful and indeed necessary in concentrating one's mind to the task at hand. High anxiety,

however, can be disruptive, distressing and interfere with goal-directed activities and daily functioning. Some children (and adults) are more prone to anxiety. An inhibited temperament predisposes children to anxiety and worry. The role of the family has been shown to be an important factor in shaping children's response to stress and anxiety.

The concept of 'container–contained' put forward by the psychoanalyst Wilfred Bion (1963), is a useful model in understanding anxieties in children and the role of parents in managing them. Bion drew attention to the fact that the child (Bion was referring mainly to infants) on exposure to the vicissitudes of life gets overwhelmed by feelings of high anxiety and uncontrolled emotions and feels a sense of disintegration ('falling to pieces') and panic. Unable to manage these intense painful feelings they project it onto the mother (or onto any primary care giver). A 'good enough' mother is able to pick up the child's signals of distress, absorb them without feeling overwhelmed herself, 'translate' them into specific meanings and act upon them, usually by holding the child. This usually takes the form of validating the child's experience and acknowledging the feelings the child has been experiencing, 'digesting' them and returning them to the child in a form that the child can tolerate. When this happens, the child feels understood and assured of their security and after a while is able to 'internalise the mother' and manage their anxieties better. Thus the mother acts as the 'container' for the child's unbearable feelings. On the other hand, when a mother is not attuned to the child's experiences, or when she herself is overwhelmed by the anxiety, she is unable to perform the containing function. This results in the child becoming more anxious, fearful and declining into a state of near terror. A more mundane example of parental containment may be seen in instances that generate high emotion, such as that occur when a family meets with an accident; if the parents remain relatively calm and show the children that they can manage the situation reasonably well, the children tend to feel less anxious and behave themselves. This is an example of how parents can 'contain' children's anxieties. On the other hand, if the parents panic and are overtaken by their own worries, the children too tend to 'go to pieces'.

Until now we have discussed anxiety in general. It the following section we discuss specific forms of anxieties that are common in SR. Although these conditions are described separately and as distinct entities, more often than not the picture may not be clear cut and overlap between the categories is common. Two specific forms of anxiety states commonly seen in children showing SR are separation anxiety and social anxiety (also called social phobia). The former is more common in the young child (typically under 12 years) and the latter in adolescents. These are described in some detail below. This is followed by a brief note on generalised anxiety and panic attacks, both of which may be seen in some children with SR.

Separation anxiety and separation anxiety disorder

Developmentally 'normal' separation anxiety occurs around the age of one year, during which the child experiences anxiety when separated from the main attachment figure. Separation anxiety peaks between one to three years and gradually declines, and by the time the child starts nursery and later the reception class, the child learns to be away from the parents over a longer and longer period of time. By the time children start school they have sufficiently internalised the mother to enable them to manage their anxieties about separation.

Separation anxiety disorder is characterised by developmentally inappropriate and excessive anxiety upon separation or anticipation of separation from home or from those to whom the child is attached. The hallmark of the disorder is extreme fear and distress at the time (or in anticipation) of separation from the mother. SR is a prominent feature of the disorder in middle childhood. In young children with the disorder clingy behaviour is common. Often they follow the mother everywhere in the house ('shadowing'). They have a fear of sleeping alone and come up with various excuses to sleep in the parent's bed or get the mother to come to their room. In middle childhood they are unwilling to sleep away from home. They may express fears of getting kidnapped or getting killed. They worry about the safety of the mother or some harm befalling her. When anticipating separation from the mother, they may plead, throw tantrums, threaten self-harm or become aggressive. The main features of social anxiety disorder are summarised below:

- unrealistic worry about parent (e.g. some harm befalling the major attachment figure)

- unrealistic and excessive worry that something catastrophic may happen to self resulting in separation from major attachment figure (e.g. kidnapping, getting lost, being killed)

- persistent fear of being alone, clinginess, reluctance to sleep unless close to the major attachment figure

- excessive distress during (or in anticipation of) separation from the major attachment figure

- physical symptoms of anxiety (e.g. nausea, vomiting, abdominal pain) on separation from the attachment figure.

The onset of the disorder is most commonly during middle childhood (7–12 years) with marked decline in onset during adolescence and young adulthood. Difficulties in separation–individuation may occur for a number of reasons and these may not be evident initially. Parents do not volunteer such information and, in many instances, they may be consciously unaware of them. The following account by a school nurse about an 11-year-old girl illustrates the features of separation anxiety disorder.

Kay

At the start of this school year Kay commenced at the secondary school. On the first day of school, at the time of leaving home, she was physically sick and had diarrhoea and kept saying that she could not go to school. She was taken to school by her mother, but once at school she complained of stomach ache and was unable to go into many of her lessons. Although thereafter she continued to attend school with some difficulty, after the half-term holidays she experienced the same problems of diarrhoea and stomach ache and was hysterical in the mornings. When at school Kay had been unable to attend all lessons and would sit in the nurse's room or library. She complains of headaches, feeling sick and dizzy. She becomes very distressed and wants to come home. During the half term the class went on a school trip but Kay was unable to go because she did not want to leave the family.

Kay is a sporty person and has been in the netball team at the new school but she is unable to get on the coach with the rest of the team when they go out for matches. If her mother picks her up and takes her to the matches, she is fine. She refuses to attend birthday parties of her friends unless her father or mother stay with her. However, she will stay overnight with her grandparents. Kay has difficulty in sleeping and has had nightmares. She expresses fears of being alone and has panics or tantrums at the time of separation from her parents. She is afraid of going upstairs on her own and will not go to bed unless there was someone upstairs. She will not take herself to the toilet during the night without her mother or father watching her go across the landing area. She wants the landing light switched on all night.

Social anxiety disorder (social phobia)

Social anxiety is extremely common in adolescents. In studies on community samples of youth aged 12 to 17 years more than 50 per cent of adolescents report social anxiety for at least one social situation. Whereas 'normal' social anxiety is common, transient and short lived, in a minority of young people it can be severe and disabling. When the anxiety in social situations is excessive, unreasonable and impairing it is called social anxiety disorder or social phobia.

Social anxiety disorder is a fear of being scrutinised, evaluated or being at the centre of attention. However, the real underlying fear is that the person will be evaluated *negatively* ('they will laugh at me'; 'they will think I am stupid'; 'they won't like me'; etc.). People with social anxiety disorder fear that others will find fault with them or think that they are incompetent or strange. They believe that whenever they are being looked at by others or when there is a chance that they may be attracting attention, they are at risk of being judged badly. For the person with social anxiety disorder feared situations include public speaking, parties, standing in line, using the phone when others are around, eating in public and starting a conversation. One study that examined the prevalence of social anxiety disorder in preadolescents showed that the commonest social fears related to: reading aloud in front of the class, musical or athletic performance, joining in conversations, speaking to adults, starting a conversation and writing on the blackboard (Beidel, Turner and Morris 1999). The main features of social anxiety disorder are summarised below.

- The individual experiences persistent and excessive fear of one or more social situations in which the person is exposed to people.

- The individual feels that he or she is under scrutiny or evaluation by others.

- Exposure to such social situations produces excessive anxiety which may take the form of physical symptoms, extreme apprehension and panic attacks; anticipatory anxiety is common.

- The person fears that they may act in ways that are humiliating or embarrassing; making a spectacle of oneself, vomiting, blushing or shaking.

- Avoidance of the feared situation is a prominent feature, leading to significant social and educational impairment (such as restricted friendships and SR).

Beidel, Turner and Morris (1999) identified the following types of social situations feared by preadolescent children (7–13 years) with social phobia:

- reading aloud in front of the class

- musical or athletic performance

- joining in conversations

- speaking to adults

- starting a conversation

- writing on the blackboard

- ordering food in a restaurant

- attending birthday parties

- taking tests

- answering a question in class

- working or playing with other children

- asking teacher for help

- using school or public bathroom

- inviting a friend home

- eating in the school canteen

- answering or talking on the telephone

- eating in front of others.

Excessive social anxiety can cause considerable impairment in the individual's social, academic and occupational functioning. For instance, children and adolescents with the disorder may avoid taking classes that require public speaking, joining extra-curricular activities or interacting with strangers; they also avoid social gatherings which prevents them from making friends. The social avoidance also prevents them from dating, making friends, participating in sports, speaking up in class and joining social or academic groups. Consequently youth with social phobia meet age-specific developmental challenges such as employment and dating later than their peers. Moreover, they are generally submissive in peer relationships and are viewed by them as being likely targets for ridicule, isolation and bullying. The following description of Zoe, a 15-year-old girl, is typical of social anxiety:

Zoe

Zoe had not been to school for five months. When visited by the EWO her mother told her that Zoe refused to answer the door or answer the telephone; she was unable to go out of the house and was terrified of meeting people her own age. Her problems began when she got worried six months ago about doing PE and complained of headaches. She had been complaining that she is made to read to the class and being 'put on the spot' by teachers. Academically she was advanced, especially in English. She had been excused from taking part in PE because of difficulties in changing with other girls. Then she stopped going to school altogether.

On reflection her mother felt that things had started going wrong over the preceding two years. She had started wanting to go to the cinema very late, to the 10.00 pm show so that she would be less likely to meet people. Although she likes McDonald's, she would not go in and wanted her mother to use only the drive thru. She had not gone to her granddad's 65th birthday party. She refused to go to the hairdresser and hadn't had her hair cut for a long time. Zoe is terrified of meeting others, especially those of her age group. Apart from close family members she refuses to meet others. On the few occasions her mother and aunt had taken her out shopping, Zoe had come out with a hood over her head and been hypervigilant and been on the lookout, in case she came face to face with other young people. She had been asking her mother to move to a new area, far away from where they have been living for the past twenty years. She feels she may be able to make a new start. Her mother has had her doubts about this course of action. She had recently taken Zoe on holiday to Blackpool. Zoe had been enthusiastic and been looking forward to going. She was sure that she would not meet any known people. But, once in Blackpool she had become anxious about going out and when coaxed by her mother to join her, she had had a panic attack. She felt that other people were looking at her and scrutinizing her. She spent most of the time in the hotel watching television. On returning home, she had become more self-conscious and refused to go out. When visitors came home, she would run into her room and lock the door. Her only 'friend' was a boy from the neighbourhood who was five years younger than her. She played computer games with him. But she had been complaining that she was envious of other young people whom were 'out there having fun'. This made Zoe quite depressed and miserable. Ultimately, she decided to seek help from a family friend who was a mental health nurse and was referred to CAMHS.

Generalised anxiety

In many children (and adults) the anxieties can take the form of excessive worry and apprehensive expectation that the person finds difficult to control. These worries are persistent but may wax and wane. Usually the anxiety or worry is associated with restlessness, feeling on edge, irritability, difficulty concentrating and other physical symptoms of anxiety. In short, the anxiety is not focused on separation from parents, social situations or other events, but is generalised and 'free floating'. Moreover, it is present most of the time and is not specific to particular situations. Generalised anxiety is distinguished from everyday worries by its severity and persistence as well as the marked impairment in social, educational and recreational domains. In some instances it may manifest as SR.

Panic attacks

Panic refers to a sudden and discrete period of intense fear or severe anxiety lasting usually for a few minutes only. There can be a sudden onset of palpitations, choking, sweating, shaking and dizziness together with a secondary fear of dying, losing control or going mad. It often results in a hurried exit and avoidance of similar situations and may be followed by a persistent fear of another attack. Panic attacks may occur in any anxiety state but are uncommon in children with SR, though many report periods of very high anxiety bordering on panic.

The case of Ben, continued

Mrs Leahy involved the school health advisor, Mrs Saunders, to help her with managing Ben's difficulties. She wanted her to see Ben on his own to in order to get Ben's perspective of the difficulties. When Mrs Saunders met with Ben initially he had been reticent and not forthcoming. Through sensitive questioning she found out that Ben experienced abdominal colic and severe apprehension at the time of leaving for school. His worries started the night before and he kept awake at night thinking of the ordeal he would go through the next morning. In the mornings, he would delay getting washed and dressed. At the time of leaving home he felt sick and had abdominal pain and diarrhoea. He would start getting hot and flushed and begin to shake. Mrs Saunders noticed that while talking of his morning experience, his legs were shaking and his face was flushed and he kept wringing his hands. The anxiety was worst when he had to enter the school and on the few occasions he was able to get to class and remain there, he felt better after 30 minutes or so. At weekends and school holidays he said he had no problems and it was the thought of going to school that got him upset and distressed. He was at a loss to explain why he had these difficulties.

On further inquiry (on a subsequent occasion) Ben confided in Mrs Saunders that he often worried about his mother while at school. He was sure that something terrible was going to happen to her. 'She might get badly ill and be admitted to hospital or meet with an accident and die,' he said. He had visions of her in hospital intensive care ward with bandages all over her body. When questioned about the chances of her meeting with an accident or falling seriously ill, he agreed that it was highly unlikely, but, all the same he could not stop worrying when away from home. Mrs Saunders came to the realisation that it was not the thought or act of attending school that brought on the anxiety, but the prospect of separation from his mother that made Ben so distressed.

This was later confirmed by his mother. The problem appeared not to be confined to school attendance. He had difficulties sleeping on his own and being away from his mother. He constantly checked where she was and, if she was late coming home after shopping he would get very distressed and frightened. He worried about her health and on one occasion insisted on going with her when she went to see the doctor.

The first three chapters have examined various aspects of SR, the factors that contribute to SR and anxiety and its different manifestations in children who show SR. In the next chapter we discuss how this knowledge can inform us in assessing children with SR.

Summary points

- Anxiety is a normal reaction to stressful situations, but may become disabling if excessive or disproportionate to the demands of the situation.

- Severe anxiety manifests as emotional, behavioural and physical features; close attention to details of the history and presentation are necessary in order to identify anxiety in school refusers (see Table 3.1, p.42).

- In spite of the extreme distress produced by severe anxiety, the natural course of anxiety, in any given situation, is that the level of anxiety increases rapidly, reaches a plateau over a period of about 30 minutes or so and declines thereafter (see Figure 3.3b, p.46).

- In SR, avoidance of the anxiety provoking situation, i.e. school, is the (maladaptive) coping method utilised by the child. This results in an avoidance–reinforcement cycle that over time becomes self-perpetuating (see Figure 3.2, p.44).

- The two commonest forms of anxiety seen in school refusers are separation anxiety and social anxiety; the former is more common in the younger child and the latter in adolescents. However, mixed anxiety states are common.

4 Assessment

A proper assessment of the situation and circumstances regarding SR is an essential first step before planning any interventions. It is all too tempting to plan strategies for returning the child to school without first gaining an understanding of the various aspects of the problem. Not many adults would want to attempt to resolve a personal problem without first understanding the most salient aspects. Yet it is all too common to treat SR as a trivial 'blip' and attempt a quick 'fix' by getting the child back to school as quickly as possible. Such attempts are usually based on oversimplification of the problem ('He is trying it on') or the desire to minimise the issues ('a passing phase') or to produce immediate results ('Get Jack back to school on Monday'). These actions are usually based on implicit and unacknowledged assumptions on the part of practitioners and a poor understanding of SR, or may be driven by time constraints ('I have better things to do') or lack of clarity of roles ('It is not my job').

From the preceding chapters it should be clear that the issues involved in SR cover a wide range of problems from relatively minor to highly complex. Whereas in many cases the issues may prove to be straightforward (e.g. reluctance or refusal to attend following a short illness), in others the situation may be exceedingly complex, with persistent absence from school, long-standing family problems and intractable difficulties at school. It is important that even in what appears to be 'simple cases' a systematic approach is adopted so that most aspects of the case are examined before a plan of return to school is implemented. Thus assessment, however simple, should precede intervention.

Having decided to carry out an assessment, the practitioner is faced with a series of who? where? what? questions. That is, who should take main responsibility for addressing the problem, where the assessment should be carried out and what needs to be done? SR comes to the attention of a number of professionals and practitioners; initially it is the form teacher, the head teacher and perhaps the special needs co-ordinator (SENCo) who are concerned. They may bring it to the attention of the education welfare officer (EWO), education psychologist (EP), school health advisor or school nurse (SHA) and in some cases social services, child and adolescent mental health services (CAMHS) and child health services too may be involved. In general, in the vast majority of instances of SR frontline professionals who already know the child and family, i.e. the teachers, are best placed to take the lead in devising interventions. In some local education authorities the SHAs and EWOs may take an active part in dealing with SR. The following account of assessment and management is based on the assumption that in most cases frontline educational professionals are best suited for the purpose of identifying, assessing and intervening. There is little doubt that for interventions to be successful the school should take the initiative not only in identification of school refusal but also in the analysis of the situation and formulating interventions. In this they will no doubt require the assistance of other services and professionals (see Chapter 8 for a discussion on the role of schools).

Dealing with families and children requires time and space. Schools often have difficulty in finding offices or rooms where the family and child can be seen in privacy. It is important to be able to make the place welcoming and as safe and private as possible. Many teachers and SHAs may prefer to make a series of home visits. Most practitioners are aware of the need to take a friendly, professional and confidential approach towards the work and are often guided by the code of practice by their respective professions. They are aware of the need to be respectful and sensitive towards the children and families. The commonest pitfall that awaits the practitioner dealing with school refusers is the tendency to be judgemental of the child or family. Blaming the child ('he is ... putting it on/lazy/controlling') or the family ('they are weak/colluding with the child/not interested') is all too easy, especially when faced with a persistent school refuser. Practitioners need to include themselves in the system that they are working with and be prepared to examine their own attitude, motivation and feelings evoked by the case. The first principle in working with children and families is to try to be as objective as possible while at the same time being empathetic and understanding. Professional supervision is a useful but a rare resource.

The main aims of assessment are:

1. to confirm that it is indeed a case of SR as opposed to truancy or parentally condoned absence

2. to assess the extent and severity of (a) school absence, (b) anxiety and (c) ascertain the type(s) of anxiety

3. to gather information regarding the various child, family and school factors that may be contributing to the SR in a given child

4. to integrate the available information to arrive at a practical working hypothesis as a prelude to planning effective interventions.

In dealing with SR it is useful to think in terms of triangles or triangular relationships, i.e. the assessment should be informed by the reciprocal relationship between the child, the family and school. The assessment process usually begins with an interview with the family and child (the child needs to be seen individually at some point) followed by an interview with the teacher most involved with the child. But the interviews may be carried out in any order and by a single worker or two or more workers. All throughout the assessment interviews it is useful first to get a description (the what? question) of the presenting problem *before* exploring the possible reasons for it (the why? questions). A specimen assessment form is given in Appendix II.

Family (parental) interview

The family interview takes the form of a friendly meeting with the parents and the identified child. Some prefer to see the whole family including siblings; others may opt to see only the parents and the school refusing child while some practitioners may want to spend time with parents alone. Although time consuming, meeting the family in their own territory through home visits is an excellent way of starting off the process of assessment.

During the first family interview, following introductions and explanation of the reasons for the meeting, it is useful to begin with first getting a *behavioural description* of the school refusing behaviour. What this means is that one must strive to get an objective and measurable description of the pattern of SR: the frequency, pattern, duration and pattern of SNA. Next, it is useful to explore the history of the problem, its onset and the course of its development. What were the first indications of the difficulties? When was it first observed? Were there similar problems previously in the primary school? This should be followed by obtaining an accurate description of the child's behaviour at the time of going to school, paying special attention to features of anxiety (see Chapter 3). Getting a description of the child's 'typical day', including getting ready in the morning, who takes the child to school and how he or she is during the rest of the day is one useful way of gathering information. It is also useful to ask how the child spends his or her time when not at school. Asking each parent's for a description of the child's personality (parents love to talk about this), his or her strengths, hobbies and social life is helpful in order to get a well-rounded picture of the child as a person. Here are some questions to ask the parents:

- Can you describe as best as you can how your child is when he or she has to go to school?

- Does your child tell you what makes school scary for him or her?

- Can you describe a 'typical day' from the time he or she gets up and goes to (or doesn't go to) school?

- What does your child do when he or she is not at school? What do other family members do?

- In your view why do you think your child had difficulties attending school? (Ask this question of each parent individually. If one parent is not present ask, 'What does your husband/wife make of it?')

- Who in the family is better at dealing with the situation? Why?

- Have there been any recent changes or events in the family that may have contributed to the problem?

- As far as you are aware has your child had problems with schoolwork, peers or teachers?

Getting the parents or the child to help draw their family tree (also called a genogram) and discussing 'who is like whom' is a useful way of engaging the family as well as obtaining background information about the family. Any recent changes in the family (including bereavements, separations, house moves) and stresses should be noted. Enquiring about their beliefs about the reason for the school refusal may provide important insights into the parent's ideas of the issues involved and provide an opening for future work with them. Finding out about their relationship with school (and particular teachers) and the methods they had already tried to overcome the problem are important to get a full picture of the situation. Curiosity about why the problem had occurred at this point in time may get the practitioner to think about the various family factors that may have contributed to the problem.

Child interview

Talking to the child on his or her own about personal and family issues raises several ethical and moral issues. Parental permission is usually necessary before formally interviewing the child. Most secondary school children may be willing to be seen on their own. When children are reluctant to be seen on their own, it is best to see them with their parents. As a group school refusers present as shy, timid and anxious individuals. Communicating with such children may initially be difficult, especially when they may feel you are there to force them into attending school. Getting to know them as persons in their own right and as individuals inhabiting a world of football, video games, Ipods and mobile phones is one way of establishing rapport. Indirect approaches such as drawing and play are less anxiety provoking and help connect with the young person.

Phrasing the questions in a developmentally appropriate way, following the child's lead and using open-ended questions are useful ways of communicating with children. One of the aims of the child interview is to get an accurate description of the physical and emotional experiences of the child at the time of going to school. This is best done through asking open-ended questions: 'Tell me what it is like for you in the morning?', 'I want to know exactly what you go through in the mornings; can you share it with me?', are helpful ways of approaching the subject. Some children may not be able to say exactly what it is that causes the fear of going to school and may have to be helped to think about it rather than suggesting answers or having words put into their mouths. Many young children lack a vocabulary to describe their experience of anxiety and may use words like 'scary', 'jittery' or 'upset'. After getting a personal account of the symptoms in the morning it is necessary to explore the various features of anxiety that may be present by systematic questioning ('When some people are upset, they may feel sick, sweat a lot or shake, do you experience any of these things?'). Making use of the child's language to describe the problem (after obtaining a description of the thoughts, feelings and behaviour associated with the problem) is a good way of assigning a name to the problem. For example, when asked what name he would give his difficulties in attending school, a 10-year-old boy called it 'the morning bug'. A typical child interview may involve the following questions:

- Do you get nervous or scared when you have to go to school/when in school?

- Can you describe how it feels to you when you have to go to school?

- Are you scared of certain things or is it more like you are worried about everything about school?

- What exactly is that makes the school scary for you?

- Is there anything about the school that bothers you a lot that may help me understand why you have trouble attending school (e.g. bullying, difficulties with lessons)?

- Can you describe a typical day from the time you wake up to the time you are in school (or not)?

- Can you give me the 'temperature' reading at each of these times? (Introduce the Fear Thermometer (Figure 4.1) before asking this question). Alternatively, you may want to give a list of situations (e.g. being away from parents, having to talk in front of class) and ask the child to give 'temperature' ratings for each.

- What do you say to yourself when you feel fearful or scared? What are your nervous thoughts?

- What does your mother/father do when you refuse to go to school?

A technique that has been found to be helpful in building a picture of the child's various fears and anxieties is the use of the 'fear thermometer'. Essentially this is a visual analogue scale on which the child rates his or her anxiety on a scale of 0 to 100 where zero is no anxiety and 100 is extreme fear (in younger children a scale 0 to 10 may be used). The children are asked to rate their 'scariness' at each step of going to school from getting ready to going into the classroom. Young children may need help with drawing the thermometer while older children may find the concept easy to grasp. This gives a picture of the course of anxiety levels over the school day. In the case of young people who show considerable social anxiety, it may be informative to ask the reading on the fear thermometer when facing stressful situations in school such as answering questions, writing on the board, eating in public, and so on.

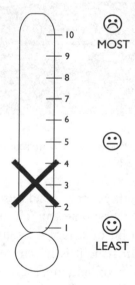

Figure 4.1 The fear thermometer used by children to rate the degree of fear. The X indicates the degree of anxiety at a particular time and place

Another way of opening up a dialogue with the child is do a 'home to school' drawing exercise. This involves getting the child to draw the way from home to school and get the child to give a running commentary about the thoughts and feelings that he experiences (including the 'temperatures' at various points in the journey) from the time he leaves home to the time he settles down in class. Young children enjoy drawing their school and explaining the lay out the place and the associated difficulties. Figure 4.2 shows one such drawing by a 12-year-old girl with severe SR.

Figure 4.2 Drawing of school by a 12-year-old girl with school refusal. The school is perceived as an unsafe and dangerous place

Next the context to the difficulties may be addressed through open-ended questions ('When was the first time you felt like this?', 'Tell me a little more about it' and 'What bit of school do you dislike most, what comes next?'). If bullying is an issue it is important to get a detailed account of the type and frequency of bullying. Many children find it difficult to discuss the subject of bullying at length. This is because they feel so humiliated about allowing the bullying to happen, so it is a second humiliation if they have to admit it. One way of overcoming the resistance to talk about bullying is to administer a questionnaire that covers all aspects of verbal, physical and relational bullying. Young children may want it read to them while older children find filling the questionnaire impersonal and easy. The Olweus bullying/victim questionnaire

(Olweus 1994) is a useful tool in this respect. It is a 40-item self-rating scale and is intended for use in children from 8 to 16 years.

Issues about difficulties with particular lessons, keeping up with school work and other anxieties associated with lessons should be explored. For professionals who may not know about the child's attainment at school, the meeting with the child or young person also provides an opportunity for a rough assessment of his or her level of intelligence and reading and writing abilities. These initial impressions may need to be confirmed by reports from school or specific psychological tests.

In-depth assessment of the child's difficulties may need several sessions especially when addressing the possibility of specific types of anxieties such as separation anxiety and social anxiety. The main features of these two conditions were discussed in Chapter 3. The following is a list of questions aimed specifically at eliciting features of separation anxiety and social anxiety:

- Do you find it difficult to be away from your mother/parents/ home?

- Have you had 'sleep-overs' with friends or other members of the family?

- What are the sleeping arrangements at home? Do you sleep in your own bed?

- Can you describe the thoughts that go through your mind when you have to be away from your mother/parents/home?

- When you are away from home do you worry that something terrible will happen to your mother, father or family?

- When you are away from home do you worry that something terrible will happen to you or some harm will come to you?

- When you get upset at leaving home/parents, what sort of experiences do you have (ask for detailed description of symptoms of anxiety)?

- Do you ever worry that other children or people will in some way judge you negatively or think badly of you?

- Are there any situations or activities that you avoid or would like to avoid because you worry about what people will think of you?

- What sorts of things do you worry about if you enter those situations?

- In what way does your worry about what people think of you stop you from doing things that are important to you?

Teacher report

Discussion with the teacher who knows the child best or the one who has been most involved with the child is essential in order to understand the problem in the school context. Additionally, teachers have a wealth of information about the children they teach and the opinions of experienced teachers are invaluable.

In SR a close examination of attendance record over a period of time is fundamental to getting to grips with the problem. It helps to understand the extent and pattern of loss of schooling and reveal absences that may have been authorised for supposedly medical reasons. At times the attendance rates may have been near normal, but the child may not have been in class and the teacher will be able to tell whether this was a problem associated with difficulties remaining in class. Figure 4.3 provides a specimen school attendance record.

Week beginning	Mon	Tue	Wed	Thu	Fri
04/09/2006	I I	/ I	/\	/\	/\
11/09/2006	L\	/\	/\	/\	/\
18/09/2006	/\	L\	/\	/\	/\
25/09/2006	L\	/\	I I	I I	I I
02/10/2006	O O	/\	/\	/\	/\
09/10/2006	I I	/ I	/\	/\	/\
16/10/2006	I I	I I	/\	/\	/\
23/10/2006	I I	/\	/\	/\	I I

Summary:	Sessions	%
Attendances	195	66%
Authorised absences	95	33%
Unauthorised absences	2	0.2%
Possible attendance	292	

Key: /: Present AM; \: Present PM; I: Illness; L: Late; O: Unauthorised absence

Figure 4.3 An example of a school attendance record (only a part of the record is shown)

Furthermore, a description of the child's behaviour before and after the onset of the problem, any signs of anxiety witnessed by the teacher and the various attempts made by the teacher to help the child are very useful pieces of information. A general description of the child's personality, peer relationships and strengths and difficulties are helpful in gaining a picture of the child. The teacher may also be able to tell the worker about any learning difficulties, results of SATs and any changes in class settings. Finally, meeting (or telephoning) the teacher provides an excellent opportunity to begin a working relationship with the teacher. Some useful questions to ask the teacher are:

- How well do you know X?

- How would you describe X? What are X's strengths and weaknesses?

- Do you feel that he or she is being subjected to bullied or treated unfairly?

- How would you describe X's academic abilities (average/above average/below average)?

- Are there known or possible (general or specific) learning difficulties?

- Have you observed any emotional difficulties in him/her at school? If so, what have these been?

- How does he or she get along with peers?

- Does he or she enjoy school?

- What is your understanding of his/her school attendance problems?

Alternatively, the worker may want to obtain a written report (with permission from the parents) or send them a pre-prepared school report form to complete.

Integration of information

At the end of the assessment process the practitioner will have in his or her possession a vast quantity of information about the child, family, school and the various difficulties. Any information is useful only to the extent that relevant aspects of it are linked together to make sense and give meaning. The formulation needs to go beyond the 'symptoms' in the child (e.g. anxiety) to include the interactional elements perceived in the context of the problem. Making a coherent formulation of the problem in interactional terms is an essential prerequisite for developing a management plan. Albert Einstein once said, 'The formulation of a problem is far more essential than its solution, which may be merely a matter of mathematical or experimental skill.' Although, to lesser mortals than Einstein, the solution to SR problems may be as challenging as the formulation of the problem, the importance of making a formulation cannot be overemphasised.

It is important to remember that in their day-to-day work all practitioners are constantly making formulations. These may be rudimentary ('I feel Jack is frightened of bullies') or straightforward ('Jack had difficulties separating from his mother; I wonder what makes him feel that way?'). Nonetheless, formulations they are. As the practitioner comes to understand the various factors contributing to SR more complex and meaningful formulations can be made. One way of thinking about it is to work out the various child, family and school factors that cumulatively cause or maintain the problem. Figure 4.4 provides an example of a diagrammatic representation of a formulation. Although the various contributory factors are shown to be independent of one another and the direction of causality unidirectional for the sake of simplicity, as will be explained later (see Chapter 5) an interaction approach to the problem is more useful than a list of risk factors, both to make sense of the issues and devise strategies for interventions.

Three aspects of the formulation must be emphasised:

1. In any given case of SR some factors may be more important than others.

2. All formulations are no more than hypotheses and the practitioner must be prepared to revise, modify or even discard them, if necessary.

3. It should be acknowledged that there are many different ways of understanding a given case and alternative formulations are possible, and may indeed be necessary.

The three activities of assessment–formulation–intervention are not separate processes; they are interlinked in a circular fashion. Moreover,

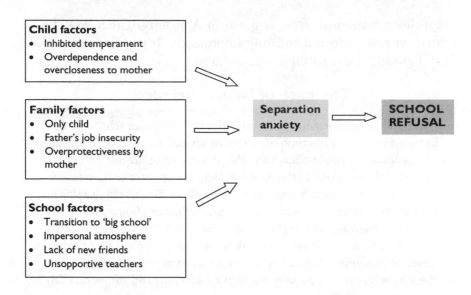

Figure 4.4 Diagrammatic representation of the initial formulation of Ben's school refusal

they are continuous processes that influence one another in a reciprocal way. For example, during the period of intervention new information may emerge that makes one reassess the initial formulation and devise different interventions. Figure 4.5 illustrates the relationship between assessment, formulation and intervention.

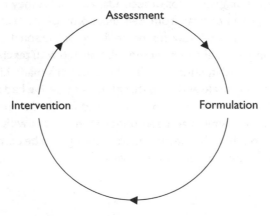

Figure 4.5 Relationship between the three steps of assessment, formulation and intervention

A specimen assessment form is given in Appendix II that provides a format for collecting and collating information. It is meant to be used flexibly to suit the needs of the practitioner.

The case of Ben, continued

Ben's difficulties in attending school fit the description of school refusal. Extreme anxiety at the time of attending school, absence of anxiety at weekends and school holidays and the absence of behaviour difficulties point to school refusal as the main problem. He appears to have severe degree of separation difficulties as shown by his difficulties in sleeping in his own bed, clinginess to his mother and difficulties being away from home on sleep-overs and school trips. His separation worries centred around some harm befalling the family especially his mother. At other times he was worried about his safety when away from his mother. On the whole he saw the outside world as threatening and dangerous. On the positive side, Ben was an intelligent boy who liked school and was keen to attend school. He was sociable and popular in class and was well liked by the teachers.

He was the only child in the family and appeared to be over close to his mother. Moreover, his father appeared less involved with Ben, partly because of his long working hours. Mrs Saunders, the SHA, wondered whether his mother too had difficulties in separation from Ben and made a mental note to explore it further with Mrs Taylor at an appropriate time. Ben had shown difficulties in separation from her when he started at the primary school and the transition to secondary school had been an important factor in the onset of his school refusal. He had been finding the ethos of secondary school somewhat daunting. She was surprised to hear from Ben that some of the teachers in the 'new school' did not know his name. Lack of personal attention at school, the impersonal nature of the relationship with teachers and the difficulties staff had in understanding his problems made him perceive the school as an unsafe and even threatening place. He had not formed new friends in the school as none of his old friends had moved to his new school. The family had been under some stress with his father's insecurity about his job. The main factors thought to be contributing to Ben's school refusal are shown in Figure 4.4.

Summary points

- Distinguishing SR from other causes of SNA can be difficult. Awareness of the features of anxiety associated with school attendance is the key to identification of SR.

- A sensitive approach to understanding the problem without prejudging the child (as lazy or wilful) or the family (blaming or pathologising) is essential in understanding SR.

- An initial assessment should involve systematic interviews with the family, child and information from school.

- Identifying the child, family and school factors that contribute to the onset and maintenance of the SR problem is an essential step in the assessment process.

- It is essential to make an integrated formulation of the problem before embarking on interventions.

5 Principles of Intervention and Management

The aim of intervention in school refusal is not *only* return to school. This may seem somewhat paradoxical. As pointed out in previous chapters, the long-term consequences of SR can be very grave, especially when the SR is severe and prolonged. In addition to the obvious educational implications, the handicaps resulting from prolonged SR can prove to be highly disabling, resulting in severe social and emotional impairment. The most damaging aspect of prolonged SR is that it impedes the development of normal, age-appropriate levels of independence, especially separation from parents and/or development of peer relationships. As Gardner has pointed out, 'These children are not simply fearful of their long list of objects and situations. Rather, they are basically afraid of life. The world for them is, indeed, a dangerous place and they feel themselves helpless to cope with all the menacing forces that lie in await for them' (1992). SR is often the first sign of future difficulties for the child; when managed well the child is able to overcome the problems and develop in other social, emotional and behavioural domains as well.

Proper management of SR helps the child overcome the disabling effect of anxiety and is therefore crucial in facilitating age-appropriate independence and in developing coping strategies. Many professionals may not realise that successful and sustained return to school and attention to factors that contribute to the SR is *the* treatment of the anxiety associated with SR. Many children, particularly those with mild to moderate forms, do not need other forms of 'treatment'. Details of *how* it should be managed and, more importantly, *who* should take primary responsibility for management are matters for the agencies and professionals involved to decide. At present, there is little agreement in educational circles as to how this is best carried out. Issues related to how the programme of management could be organised are dealt with in Chapter 9. In the following section we discuss the main *principles* that underlie the management of SR.

A joint system approach to the problem

The concept of systems and systemic thinking is an extremely useful way of viewing the problem of SR (and, for that matter, most other difficulties). A system is defined as an entity that maintains its existence through mutual interaction of its parts. The key emphasis is on 'mutual interaction'. Note that systems thinking, also called systemic thinking, is not the same as systematic thinking. Some of the features of systemic thinking will now be discussed.

Context

'Thinking systemically' means studying and treating problems within the context(s) in which they occur. It is not possible to do this with just one person presenting with the problem. Every individual is embedded in multiple contexts – physical, cultural and relationship contexts. Understanding individuals and their troubles is a matter of understanding them within, not separate from, their contexts. Thinking systemically means studying and treating problems within the context(s) in which they occur. Regardless of the group one is working with it is imperative to have a clear understanding of the systems involved. In SR there are, at the least, two overlapping social systems that are in dynamic interaction with each other: the school and the family (Figure 5.1). It is therefore necessary to explore the problem in the context of the family and school. The aims of addressing the problem in the dual context of family and school are as follows (Dowling and Osborne 1994):

1. to facilitate communication between school, staff and family members

2. to clarify differences in perception of the problem focusing on *how* it occurred rather than *why*

3. to negotiate commonly agreed goals

4. to explore specific steps towards change.

It is important to remember that the concept of context also applies to practitioners involved with dealing with SR.

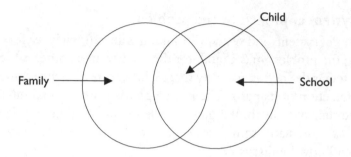

Figure 5.1 School and family system

Expanding the focus ('using the wide angle lens')

This approach necessarily shifts the focus from the individual (in our case, the child) to how the problem (SR) connects with the context(s) in which it occurs. In short, the focus moves from the child to other significant relationships, whether it be school, peer group, neighbourhood or even a (sub)culture. It is akin to using the fish eye lens rather than the zoom lens in photography. By widening the field of observation, it allows flexibility by creating the possibility of new perspectives or 'frames' within which to view the problem of SR.

Circular causality

This means that two or more individual entities influence each other in a back-and-forth fashion (represented as: A ↔ B) as opposed to linear causality (i.e. A causes B). The notion of reciprocal causality has implications for the way professionals view the problems. If causality is linear it makes sense to think of well-defined causes that lead to discrete effects (cause → effect). However, when causality is reciprocal, the roles of cause and effect oscillate as follows: A → B → C → A → B → C and so on. Thus the behaviour of one component of the system is seen as affecting and being affected by the behaviour of other parts of the system. Thus A affects B, which in turn affects C, which feeds back to affect A and so on (Figure 5.2). In such situations, it does not make sense to locate 'the cause of the problem' in one person and to view the as the effect or the result of the cause. The emphasis is on patterns of interactions that *maintain* the problematic behaviour rather than searching for 'cause'.

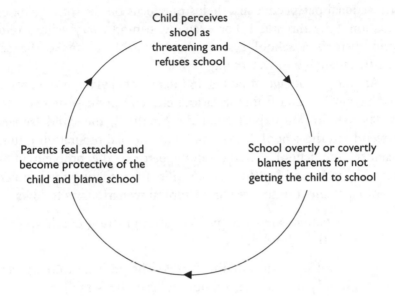

Figure 5.2 An example of circular interaction in school refusal

Interactional approach

The systemic approach is fundamentally different from the traditional analytic approach to problems. Analysing a problem involves focusing on separating the individual parts of the problem. Systemic thinking, in contrast, focuses on how things interact with each other. Thus the problem is viewed as occurring *between* people rather than *inside* a person. Decontexualised descriptions of behaviour of a school refusing child as either due to anxiety in the child (a mental health description), or difficulties in the family (e.g. uninvolved father) or problems in the school (e.g. uncaring teacher) are of little value in making sense of the behaviour or managing it. Viewing the problem in interactional terms means that none of them are totally responsible for the problem. A systemic approach thus opens up new possibilities so that interventions can be focused on areas that have the best chance of producing change. The implication of such a strategy is that participants (school and parents) carry equal responsibility for designing and implementing interventions.

Often schools 'co-operate' with interventions rather than take an active role. But dealing with school problems such as SR demands the active participation of schools in addressing the problems instead of leaving it to the 'experts' to deal with them. Observing the problem from an interactional perspective also helps one focus on the 'other side of the equation' ('the flip side'). For example, behind every school refusing child there is a school system that is unable to make the school non-threatening and welcoming.

Another advantage of taking an interactional view of the problem is that it removes blame from the various elements in the system: the family ('what else do you expect from the Smiths?'), the child (separation anxiety) and the school ('the school with the bad reputation'). In many instances the school and the family perceive the problem in linear (blaming) ways and lay the responsibility for resolving the problem on the other element in the system. A typical scenario is as follows:

1. The parents view the problem as originating in school ('If only the school did X').

2. School staff attribute the cause of the problem to the parents ('If only the mother did not mollycoddle Sarah').

3. The child gets referred to a third party (e.g. CAMHS) and the problem is understood as located in the child, the weakest member in the system.

Boundaries, subsystems, belief systems, hierarchies and power distribution

All systems (e.g. the school, the family) have their boundaries and contain subsystems (e.g. the sibling and parental subsystems within the family system) which are in constant interaction with one another. All systems have their own hierarchies along which power is distributed, their own belief systems and their subculture. Thus an understanding of the particularities of a given school and how it is organised, as well as the school refusing child's family composition and functioning are of utmost importance for anyone wanting to intervene to resolve the problem.

The observer is part of the system

It is important to realise that once a person gets involved with any system in a professional capacity he or she *automatically* becomes part of the system and is never thereafter independent of the system, whether one likes it or not, i.e. the observer too is a part of the system. In short, observer and observed cannot be separated, and the result of observations will depend on their interaction. Systemic thinking regards observation from outside a system as impossible; the act of observing makes the observer part of the system that he or she is studying. Therefore, according to systemic thinking the observer should be included in the definition of the system. In the case of SR, this means that whoever is involved with the problem – at a minimum, the school, family and the EWO – should be considered part of the system, as well as anyone else who becomes involved.

A detailed discussion of systemic principles is outside the scope of this book. For an in-depth discussion of systemic theory as applied to school settings see the review by Plas (1986). *The Family and School: A Joint Systems Approach to Problems with Children*, edited by Emilia Dowling and Elsie Osborne (1994) describes the applications of systemic thinking in school settings and is highly recommended.

Early identification

The commonest reason for the poor prognosis seen in persistent SR is delay in identification of the problem. Recognition of the problem is a prerequisite to any form of prevention or management. The longer the problems remain unaddressed, the poorer the outcome. This is especially true of SR. The longer one allows the problem to become entrenched, the more difficult it will be to get the child back to school. Although all schools have a system for monitoring school non-attendance rates, it is not uncommon for school non-attendance to go unnoticed for several months before being discovered. In Chapter 1 we outlined the main reasons for this state of affairs. Putting in place effective systems to identify SR (in addition to truancy) at an early stage requires decisions at an organisational level.

Prompt assessment

Once identified, an assessment has to be prompt. There is always a temptation to bypass the stage of assessment and get on to intervention as soon as possible. Indeed, some schools of thought do not believe in a generic assessment. Identifying the various factors contributing to refusal to attend school, however, is an essential step before embarking on interventions. This would require, at a minimum, a meeting with the parents (and child) and a member of the school staff.

Early intervention

The second commonest cause of failure in working with this group is undue delay in intervening. Any intervention has to be executed with the least amount of delay. At times this may result from delays in excluding medical reasons for the non-attendance, but often it is because there are no systems in place to address the problem of SR (see Chapter 9). There is much to be said for managing most SR problems at a school level rather than referring to other agencies. There are several compelling reasons for immediate interventions at a school level for most, if not all cases, of SR:

- Professionals already involved with the child and family and who are familiar are more acceptable to the child and family.

- The child and family are not 'singled out' for intervention by 'experts'. This is often perceived by parents as indication of severe problems. Moreover, it has the undesirable effect of pathologising the child/family whereas normalisation should be the guiding principle of interventions.

- It prevents stigmatisation, especially for the child, who has to explain it to his peers.

- It compels the school to take an active part in resolving the issue rather than merely co-operating with the intervention plan.

- Working at a school level has the potential to bring about systemic changes in schools and their ethos.

Graded return to school (desensitisation)

The cornerstone of the management of SR is the graded return of the child to school and eventual reintegration of the pupil into the class. It is of utmost importance that a Return to School Plan (RSP) is carefully constructed. For the RSP to be effective, it should fulfil the following requirements:

- It has to be well thought out and properly planned; the commonest cause of failure of a RSP is inadequate planning.

- It should be realistic; overambitious RSPs run the risk of failure and implementing a second programme is usually more difficult because of the process of sensitisation discussed in Chapter 3 (see Figure 3.3c).

- The aim should be a gradual and graded return rather than a hurried and swiftly executed one.

- It should be individualised according to the specific needs of the child; there is no fixed formula.

- It has to be agreed by a process of negotiation between an identified member of staff, the parents and the young person.

- Difficulties in implementing the RSP should be anticipated and worked through, (e.g. when recommencing school after holidays).

The RSP plan is based not just on common sense but also on sound psychological principles. The psychological knowledge base that underlies the RSP as described above is known as desensitisation. Desensitisation (also called systemic desensitisation) refers to a procedure in which the person is exposed to the feared (and avoided) situation in a gradual or graded manner, beginning with small steps. At each step the exposure is prolonged long enough to achieve habituation so that the person overcomes the fear or anxiety sufficiently before proceeding on to the next step. Essentially the three core principles of desensitisation are:

1. developing, with the collaboration of the child, a list of feared situations of increasing difficulty ('the fear ladder')

2. helping the child cope with anxiety *before* embarking on exposing him or her to the feared situation

3. practising each step daily, or as often as possible.

Applied to SR, this consists of constructing, in order of difficulty, a list (hierarchy) of situations that the child finds hard to face and planning a course of action to overcome each of them in a step-by-step fashion. In practical terms this would involve drawing up a partial or cut down time-table with the active participation of the child and the family. Paying attention to details is important at this stage to ensure successful implementation of the plan. The main aim is to get the child to face up to the previously feared (and avoided) situation long enough for the anxiety to subside at each step. When the exercise is repeated several times, with each successive exposure the level of anxiety gets progressively less until it is almost obliterated. This is known as habituation. The first few attempts are bound to be the most difficult, but the effect of repeated exposure on anxiety levels, demonstrating the desensitisation effect, is shown in Figure 5.3. The reader may want to compare it with Figure 3.3b and c in order to appreciate the principles that underlie the process.

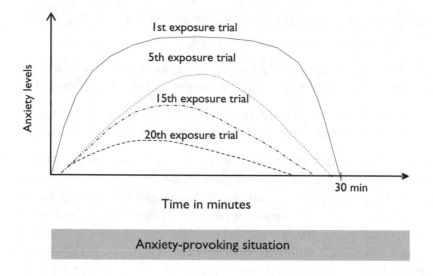

Figure 5.3 Desensitisation: Sucessive exposure to the feared situation produces gradual decline in anxiety levels (Thambirajah 2004, p.10) (compare with Figure 3.3b and c)

Involving other professionals and agencies

SR is a complex problem and it must be acknowledged that it often necessitates the provision of a range of services. While most instances of SR could be managed successfully by school and educational staff, at times it may be necessary to involve other agencies. The advantage of managing SR at the school level was discussed at the beginning of the chapter. It is worth pointing out that *routine* involvement of outside agencies may complicate the problem rather than solve it. In this respect the dictum 'if you are not part of the solution, you are part of the problem' is quite applicable to outside agencies. Other agencies such as CAMHS, as useful as they can be, may make the problem worse than it is, at least in the eyes of the child and the family, and pathologise it to an irredeemable degree. Moreover, it may have the undesirable effect of de-skilling teachers in their efforts to deal with the problem.

However, there are occasions when CAMHS may need to be involved. It is best if this is carried out according to local protocols based on good practice rather than in an ad hoc way. In general the main indications for referral to CAMHS are:

- very severe anxiety

- severe family problems (e.g. severe difficulties in separation)

- severe anxiety or mental health problems in family members

- coexisting problems, e.g. eating disorders, severe generalised anxiety

- unusual and odd behaviours in the child.

Other educational services such as pupil referral units and home tuition services may be necessary for a minority of school refusers (see Chapter 8).

Clarifying the roles of professionals involved and maintaining good communication

Whenever a number of professionals are involved it is important to be clear about the respective roles and responsibilities of each person or agency. Often roles get blurred and people may make unfounded assumptions about what the others are able to do. It is also crucial to maintain good communication. Although this is acknowledged as good practice and all directives from the government insist on it, in practice this is hard to achieve. These issues are discussed in Chapter 7 and 9.

The case of Ben, continued

The Head of the Year, Mrs Leahy, lost no time in addressing Ben's difficulties in attending school. First she made discreet enquiries about any possible bullying. There did not seem to be any evidence of it. She sought the opinions of other members of staff about Ben and was told that he was a well-liked boy who was also well behaved. There was no evidence that Ben experienced any difficulties in school work and his peer interactions were observed to be satisfactory. She had already scrutinised Ben's attendance record. One particular finding was that he was not in school on the days he had PE. Together with the SENCo she made arrangements to meet with Ben and his parents in school the following week.

In this chapter we have dealt mainly with the broad principles that underpin the management of SR. In practice, attention to details and a collaborative working relationship between educational staff and the parents in managing the problem is of utmost importance. In every case, providing support and help to parents and child is an integral part of the management plan. This is discussed in the next chapter.

Summary points

- Early detection of SR is of paramount importance to achieve successful outcomes; the longer the child is away from school the more difficult it is to get him or her back to school.

- A systemic approach to the problem, taking into consideration that at least two systems – the school and the family – are involved, is essential.

- The main principle of management in SR is to expose the child or young person to the feared situation in gradual and emotionally tolerable 'doses'(desensitisation by graded exposure) until he or she learns to overcome the anxiety and achieve full attendance.

- Interventions at school and family levels are always necessary to facilitate the process of gradual reintroduction to school and overcome factors that may be contributing to SR.

- Severe or persistent SR may require referral to CAMHS for assessment and specific treatments in addition to the above interventions.

- A small minority of severely disabled school refusers may require the services of pupil referral units and home tuition services.

- Since a number of professionals are usually involved with the child, family and the school, clarification of their respective roles and good communication are essential.

6 Working with Parents and Children

It is useful to remind ourselves that, with rare exceptions, parents of school refusing children are as much, if not more, concerned about the school non-attendance of their offspring than professionals. Most parents feel ineffectual, inadequate and guilty. Even the school refusing child is often ridden with guilt, blame and shame. Listening to both the parents and the child is an important part of the work. They have their stories to tell and hearing their concerns, worries and anxieties as well as to their version of the stories is a necessary part of the work.

Working with parents

A crucial aspect of working with parents is the attitude that teachers and other professionals adopt towards parents and the child. When parents are invited to come to meet with teachers about their child, they often bring with them much apprehension and uneasiness. Often they feel they have been 'summoned' and expect to be blamed for the child's behaviour. Parents' attitude towards the teacher and other educational authorities are usually coloured by their previous experience with teachers, authority figures and, especially, their own experience of schooling. Parents who had difficulties with teachers and schools during their own childhood are particularly prone to be defensive or suspicious. It is important to dispel their fears and angst at the very outset and pave the way for a collaborative relationship.

Yet it is important to emphasise the importance of parental responsibility for getting the child to school. The Return to School Plan (RSP) usually involves parents taking the child to school until the child can manage on his own while being supported by the teacher and the EWO.

While the responsibility for keeping the child in school once he or she is there can be shared, the role getting the child to school in the mornings should usually remain with the parents.

In working with parents the main areas of work include the following.

- Explaining SR as mostly an anxiety-based problem that most children encounter at some stage of their school carrier helps to normalise the problem. Reframing the problem as a temporary difficulty rather than an enduring 'disorder' makes it open to change. Explaining the nature of anxiety often gets parents to think of the problem from a different perspective. Many parents find a physiological explanation in which anxiety is characterised as a 'false alarm' (where the body perceives a neutral situation as a threatening one) a useful metaphor to understand anxiety-based SR.

- Negotiating the RSP with the parents and the child is by far the most important goal of the meeting. The rationale for the plan and the practicalities need discussion and agreement from both sides. The expectation should be eventual full-time school attendance except in the most severe cases. Firmness on the part of educational staff on the issue of return to school should be accompanied by flexibility on the part of school to go the extra mile to make suitable arrangements at school to make the RSP succeed. In short, school has to be seen to be doing its part to help the child (see Chapter 8).

- At the early stages of the RSP an initial upsurge of distress in the child should be expected and the parents need to manage it calmly and praise the child when he or she succeeds. Some parents (and teachers) may view pressurising these children to go to school as cruel. It is no more cruel than immunisation injections and should be seen as a necessary part of overcoming anxiety and preparing for the vicissitudes of life.

- The importance of the need for parents to work together and agree a firm and consistent approach to the child's difficulties is of utmost importance. In most cases the task of getting the child to school is entrusted solely to the mother. In the majority of instances the father's involvement is crucial to success. Getting the father or a father figure to take sufficient responsibility, especially in the initial stages of the RSP, could make the difference between success and failure. Single parents or mothers who have to manage the child on their own may need to learn to make extra efforts to be firm with the child at the time of return to school.

- Sometimes parents may have reservations about how well the school is managing the situation, or may even be critical of particular teachers. Parents need to be aware that these matters concern adults and are not to be shared with children, even unwittingly. Presenting a united front that involves both the parents and the school is important, for some children tend to exploit any weakness adults may show.

- Parents and the child need to be warned that there may be setbacks during the execution of the RSP and that if they are unable to get the child to school according to plan it is not a disaster. They should remain optimistic and get back to the plan the next day. They should be told to expect problems after school breaks and anticipate recurrence of anxiety after weekends, school holidays or illness, and appropriate preparation for recommencing school should be considered. For example, talking about school, making a visit to the school and discussing school issues without focusing on difficulties are useful ways of getting the child to think about the return to school after school holidays.

- Parents should keep close links with a key member of school staff to support the RSP and any other difficulties that may arise. Regular contact with the identified 'key worker' is essential.

- Common parental issues that interfere with RSP need to be discussed. When parents experience difficulties in taking a consistent and firm approach this needs to be addressed. Some parents may be unwittingly maintaining avoidance despite their desire to help the child. Others may be anxious themselves and find coping with the anxious child demanding. Some families may need referral to other agencies such as CAMHS.

- Sometimes parents feel a change of school is the answer to the problems, but a change of school is almost always unhelpful because the problems tend to recur in the new setting.

Guidance for parents and children explaining the nature of SR and ways of managing it is given in Appendix III. It should be emphasised that in working with parents fundamental values of the professional such as being non-judgemental, non-blaming and respectful are the basic ingredients for successful and productive outcomes.

Working with the child

First, in working with children it is important to acknowledge the child's experience of anxiety. Many children (and adults) feel that other people do not understand their personal experience of anxiety which to them appears overpowering and uncontrollable. Often the child feels that either the adults do not understand their experiences and are dismissive or that they think that the child is 'putting it on'. Those working with children need to be able to validate the child's experiences. Empathising with the child while not colluding with his or her SR behaviour is the key to working with this group of children. Second, it is useful to normalise the child's experience of anxiety, referring to it as a universal experience that both children and adults have. Drawing from previous experiences the child might have had of 'normal' anxiety, say during examinations or going to the dentist, may help them to see the current experiences as extreme manifestations of the same phenomenon. Using the metaphor of a false fire alarm to explain how the body misinterprets anxiety is often a helpful way of getting the point across to both children and parents. Promoting the use of an innocuous term (e.g. 'morning bug', 'scary feelings' and 'school jitters' and 'false alarm') to describe the anxiety experienced by the child (and remembering to use it in every conversation with the child) is often a useful way of helping the child to verbalise his or her experience.

Third, time spent on explaining the features of anxiety to the child (and parents) is time well spent indeed. Getting the child to draw a human figure and indicate where he 'feels' the anxiety most (as in Figure 3.1) is a helpful way of engaging the child in a discussion of anxiety. The following are examples of questions to explore the child's experience:

- 'It must be really scary for you, especially if you don't know what exactly is making you feel so scared. Others may find it difficult to understand. Do you find it difficult to describe it?' [Empathising with the child]

- 'Are there other times when you have had similar but less scary feelings? Do you think I (or others) may have experienced similar feelings?' [Attempt to normalise the feeling]

- 'Let us think of a word to describe what you experience when in you try to go to school. What name would you like to give it?' [Externalising the problem]

- 'When one feels X, it is common to experience …' [Explaining anxiety]

Some children, especially those of primary school age, communicate better through drawings and play rather than by conversation. The child can be asked to draw a 'home-to-school' sketch and rate his or her anxiety levels along the way to school. Figure 6.1 shows a home-to-school drawing by a 12-year-old boy: the school as seen by the child is an unfriendly and threatening place. Such props are useful in opening up channels of communication and encouraging the child to talk of his or her fears and anxieties.

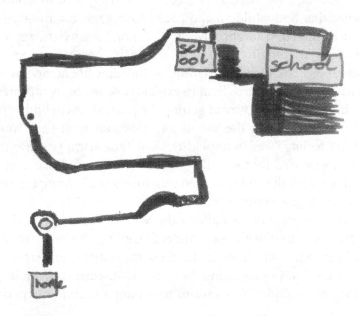

Figure 6.1 Home-to-school drawing

The fear ladder (fear hierarchy)

Another useful way of getting to know the various fears and anxieties that the child shows is to draw a 'fear ladder'. Here, with the help of the child, the worker constructs a ladder that indicates the various fears the child has in relation to school, beginning with the worst feared situation and ending with the least feared one or vice versa. This provides a pictorial representation of the child's hierarchy of fears. This is a useful tool in the planning the RSP. In the initial stages of the RSP it is important that the fears in the lower levels of the ladder are addressed and an appreciable degree of success is achieved before proceeding to the next stage, to ensure that sufficient desensitisation is produced. Moreover, it helps the child to develop a sense of success and self-efficacy. Setting up a fear hierarchy and an RSP by themselves may be insufficient unless the child is taught strategies to manage his or her insecure and anxious feelings. In short, attention has to be given to how the child can cope with his or her worries and fear of failure. An example of the fear ladder is shown in Figure 6.2.

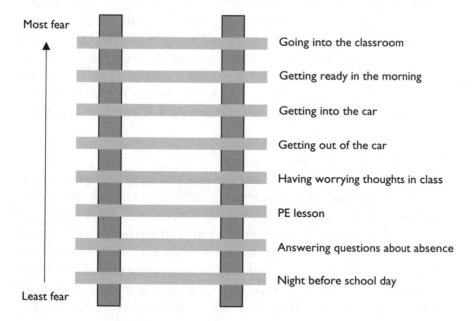

Figure 6.2 An example of a fear ladder

Coping

Coping refers to the cognitive, behavioural and affective efforts used by the individual to manage particular external or internal demands that are appraised as taxing or stressful. Three types of coping strategies have been described: solving the problem, reference to others and non-productive coping (Freydenberg and Lewis 1993). Solving the problem involves working on the problem and remaining optimistic; reference to others involves turning to others for support; and non-productive coping involves ignoring the problem, worrying and wishful thinking. School refusers typically use avoidant (non-productive) coping strategies and have low self-efficacy, i.e. they perceive themselves as lacking the capability to produce change. Getting to know the child's coping strategies in non-school related situations is one way of understanding how the child's mind works. The use of self-reported measures such as the Adolescent Coping Scale (Freydenberg and Lewis 1993) to explore how young people cope with difficult situations may shed light on their habitual ways of dealing with adversities. Encouraging them to use active problem-focused coping strategies rather than avoidant-focused coping is one way of addressing their problems. Similarly, giving attention to improving peer relationships and enhancing social skills is often necessary in instances where peer relationship problems and social anxiety issues are deemed to be important. In severe cases of SR more formal methods of intervention may be necessary. One mode of treatment shown to be effective in SR is cognitive behaviour therapy (CBT).

Cognitive behaviour therapy

This is a rather grandiloquent name given to an approach to managing feelings and behaviour by changing the self-defeating thoughts associated with them. As the name implies it consists of two components: cognitive and behavioural. The former consists of attempts to change the way the children think about themselves and the problem. The basic premise of CBT is that thoughts determine feelings and behaviour. Children with anxious SR experience intense negative thoughts at the time of setting out to school. The following thoughts are common:

- Something terrible is going to happen.

- I cannot manage to face school.

- I will collapse or faint if I get out of the car.

- I am a complete failure.

People with anxiety habitually overestimate and overgeneralise their fears and concerns and tend to make calamitous predictions. CBT approaches hold that these negative and catastrophic thoughts lead to anxious feelings and these in turn lead to avoidance behaviour. The main aim is to get the child to challenge these negative perceptions and thinking patterns and help discover ways of changing them to more positive ones.

The second, and in the case of SR the more important component of CBT, is exposure to the feared situation through a graded return to school, as discussed in the previous chapter. Direct work with the children on their perceptions and anxiety-provoking thoughts helps them to cope with the RSP more effectively. Details of CBT principles are outside the scope of this book, and the reader is referred to Graham (2005) for an introductory account.

The case of Ben, continued

In their meeting with the family and Ben, Mrs Leahy and the SENCo were able to provide information on SR and its nature. They acknowledged the real difficulties that Ben had in attending school and that they believed him. They reassured him and his family that they did not believe that he was 'not putting it on'. They discussed the principle of management (outlined in the previous chapter) and were able to develop a shared understanding of the problem. The consensus was that Ben experienced severe anxiety at separation from his parents and required help and support to face it.

Mrs Leahy negotiated a RSP with Ben and the family. Ben chose the days that he felt he could manage to attend school. He said that he found Mondays particularly difficult. On Wednesdays he had PE, a subject he disliked. After much discussion a graded return to school timetable was agreed upon. As shown in Table 6.1 the plan was to get Ben back to full-time schooling by the fourth week. Any possible barriers to implementation of the plan were discussed. Mrs Taylor was not very confident that she could get Ben to school on the days he became too distressed and kept complaining of stomach pains and feeling sick. Following some deliberation it was agreed that his father, who was better at getting Ben to attend school, would make arrangements with his workplace to take time off to take Ben to school during the first two weeks of the RSP plan. It was felt that instead of taking over from his wife the task of getting Ben to school, he would help and support her to get Ben to school. After all, he was the 'expert' in getting Ben to attend school and he would teach his wife how to manage Ben's attendance difficulties better!

Table 6.1 Initial return to school plan for Ben. During implementation of the plan the teacher came to realise that the plan was overambitious.

Week 1	Week 2	Week 3	Week 4
AM PM	AM PM	AM PM	AM PM
+ -	+ -	+ +	+ +
+ -	+ +	+ +	+ +
- -	- -	+ -	+ +
+ -	+ -	+ +	+ +
+ -	+ +	+ +	+ +

Key: + attendance; - absence

Mrs Leahy would act as the contact person for the parents and Ben was to report to her every morning when he came into school. She would provide day-to-day feedback to parents. When getting ready in the morning parents would give him some time to compose himself but on no account would the journey to school be delayed. In the rare instance where he was too distressed and they were unable to get him to school, he would always be brought to school even if it turned out to be as late as the afternoon. Mrs Leahy was to make arrangements for late attendances and he would spend some time in the library before going into the class. The aim was to make it clear to Ben, in any case, that he would be attending school according to the RSP. During the time at home when Ben was unable to make it to school he was not to be allowed television or to use the computer. Mr Taylor was to be kept informed at work by his wife about Ben's progress on a daily basis.

As a part of the RSP Mrs Saunders, the SENCo, made arrangements to meet with Ben on a biweekly basis. Initially Ben was reserved and said very little. She explained to him that she was there to support and help him and that she would keep their discussions confidential. She made it clear that she would be available whenever he had problems at school. After discussing neutral topics that included *The Simpsons* cartoon series (an interest that both of them shared), Ben was able to share his difficulties both at home and school. To Mrs Saunders he came across as an intelligent boy who was emotionally younger than his age. He was articulate but very defensive and was terrified about the external world, particularly school. She explained to him the nature of anxiety and how avoiding school and other situations that he perceived as stressful made it worse. It struck her that Ben's habitual way of dealing with stressful situations was by avoidance. For example, he did not want to think of how he could overcome the difficulties he encountered in attending school until that morning and the very last minute. Over a number of sessions she was able to teach him to use positive statements that he could repeat to himself when coming to school. Later he was taught to recognise the early signs of anxiety and to use relaxation and controlled breathing to overcome anxiety at an early stage. Mrs Saunders reflected on how well he related to her and hoped that being valued for what he was by an adult authority figure would boost his self-confidence and self-worth. Most of all she was able to instil a sense of hope and optimism by showing how well he was doing.

Working with parents and the child is necessary but not sufficient to ensure successful return to school and for overcoming anxiety. For the RSP to be successful interventions at a school level are indispensable. In the next chapter we address how the child can be supported at school and the central role schools need to play in overcoming difficulties.

Summary points

In working with parents:

- provide information about the nature of SR to the child and parents (see Appendix III)

- agree on the return to school plan (RSP)

- discuss parents' anxieties and agree on 'dos' and 'don't dos'

- help manage parents' anxieties and worries

- assist parents to take a firm and consistent approach

- get the father involved as much as possible

- impress upon them the importance of all adults (parents, educational professionals and others) working together.

In working with children:

- make time to see them individually

- ensure confidentiality

- show interest in him or her as a person and attempt to develop a relationship

- try to engage them through friendly discussion about subjects the children may be interested in

- be non-judgmental, avoid blame and reframe the problem as anxiety, adjustment difficulties or as other difficulties that can be overcome

- teach the child active coping strategies to overcome his or her anxiety.

7 Supporting Children and Young People at School

As discussed in previous chapters school attendance is a high profile issue at both national and local levels, with schools and local authorities being required to set targets for reducing non-attendance (DfEE 1999; DfES 2002) and to publish their attendance figures. In addition the DfES has taken a strategic lead in helping schools develop programmes for improving attendance through the Primary National Strategy and Key Stage 3 National Strategy. Interestingly, these strategies encourage school staff to consider the impact of school ethos and other environmental factors on attendance. While there is no specific mention of SR in the DfES guidance on attendance the focus on ethos and social and environmental aspects of schools organisations is particularly important for this group of children and young people for whom regular school attendance presents significant challenges.

In earlier chapters we examined the nature of SR and made the point that it is characterised by emotional upset, often accompanied by symptoms of excessive anxiety, with contributory factors not limited to school. In other words, for each child who exhibits SR there will be a constellation of contributory factors which may include individual child, family and school factors. The term 'school refusal' describes the behaviour: it does not attribute cause. Consequently while school factors, including the child's unique experience of school and organisational and cultural aspects of the school as an institution, may contribute to attendance difficulties the relationship between school and the child's non-attendance is unlikely to be a simple cause and effect one. Archer *et al.* (2003) used questionnaires to survey LEA and school staff across England about SR before conducting case studies in selected schools. One key finding from their research was that while school factors might 'trigger or exacerbate the problem of school refusal', school refusing behaviour would probably be symptomatic of other underlying issues. In considering the role of school in SR it may be that school constitutes a combination of risk and protective factors which interact with individual child and family factors to support or inhibit school attendance. This chapter explores this idea and looks into the role school staff may play in identifying and intervening to support children with SR.

Intervening early: Transactional risk and protective factors

Schools are complex social organisations and as such make innumerable demands on the children and young people who attend them. A cursory analysis of the demands of school life brings a new awareness of the various challenges and hurdles to be negotiated by young people on a daily basis.

Figure 7.1, developed from Roeser and Eccles (2000), is an analysis of school experience as a hierarchy of interdependent levels of organisational, instructional and social processes. It is important to note that these levels are dynamic and are negotiated between those involved in the organisation, i.e. pupil and pupil, and pupil and teachers throughout the day and week. The result is an experience of school that is interactionist in nature and in many ways unique to the individual.

The ecological–transactional model of school refusal (Figure 7.2) illustrates how contextual circumstances and within child characteristics interact to affect outcomes. At each level of the ecological system (ontogenic, e.g. child; microsystem, e.g. family, school and peers; exosytem, e.g. neighbours and local authority; and macrosystem, e.g. goverment policies) there exists risk and protective factors which have the potential to increase or decrease the likelihood of school refusing behaviour developing. Protective factors in school (microsystem) might include variables like the inclusive ethos, a senior member of staff with knowledge of SR and effective anti-bullying procedures, while risk factors might include the fact that the child is taught by 12 different teachers, none of whom knows her by name, and the fact that none of the child's friends from junior school transferred with her to this school. Some protective and risk factors will be enduring in nature while others may be transient, for example, a short illness may mean the child's only friend is absent from school for a few days. Each of these factors can affect the balance of the ecological system, with SR occurring when risk

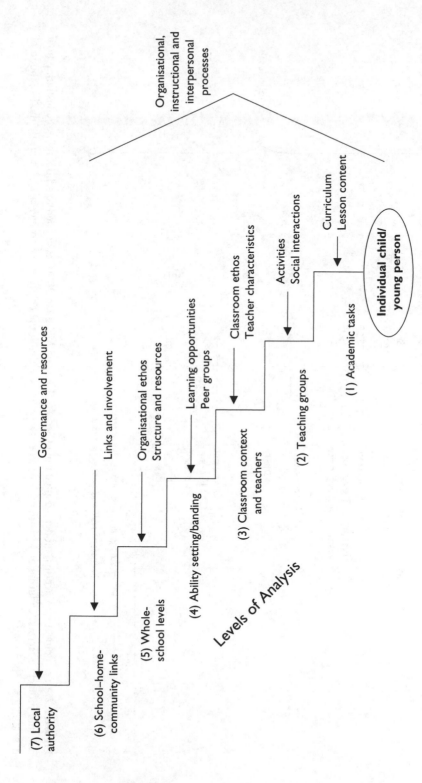

Figure 7.1 Multilevel description of school ecology (adapted from Roesser and Eccles 2000). This is a multi-level description of school ecology that represents the various complex organisational, instructional and interpersonal processes negotiated by children and young people at school

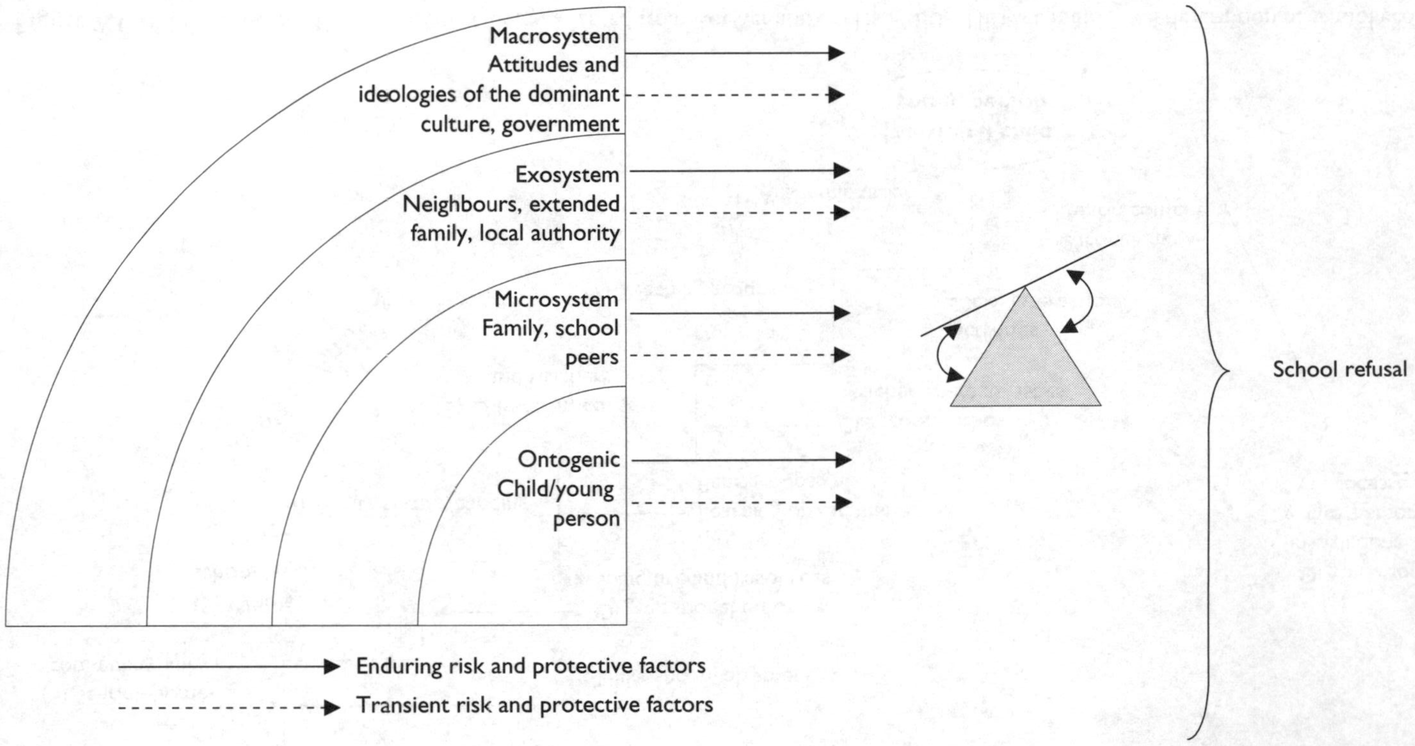
Macrosystem
Attitudes and
ideologies of the dominant
culture, government
Exosystem
Neighbours, extended
family, local authority
Microsystem
Family, school
peers
Ontogenic
Child/young
person
School refusal
Enduring risk and protective factors
Transient risk and protective factors

Figure 7.2 An ecological-transactional model (adapted from Ciccheti, Toth and Maughan 2000) as applied to school refusal, illustrating how risk and protective factors (enduring and transient) interact between the child and the environment to increase or decrease the likelihood of developing school refusal

factors outweigh protective factors. However, this imbalance might occur not only at the school level but also at the family or individual child level.

A careful analysis of risk and protective factors at each of the above levels will be necessary in order to gain a clear picture of the young person's experience of school and is a key step in intervention planning for children at risk of SR. There are many different ways of conducting such an analysis, through combinations of observation, interviews, the use of checklists, etc. but however this information is gathered the aim is to construct a multi-dimensional picture of the young person's experience of school life.

This information will then be married to information gathered about the young person as an individual and his or her family situation in order to create a holistic picture of risk and protective factors. In terms of planning school intervention the emphasis will be on addressing school factors which interact with individual child and family factors to create difficulties and identifying those factors which have the potential to protect or support positive outcomes. West Sussex County Council Educational Psychology Service (2004) has developed the profile of risk of emotionally based school refusal (EBSR) schedule, which requires practitioners to consider five key areas which are seen to be influential in the development of SR:

- loss and change
- family dynamics
- curriculum/learning issues
- social/personal (these relate largely to school issues)
- psychological/wellbeing.

School-related issues have the potential to be identified in at least four of the five key areas (excluding family dynamics). The aim in using this type of schedule is to intervene early to prevent what might appear to be relatively minor, apparently transient difficulties becoming chronic or major barriers to school attendance.

Once risk and protective factors in school and elsewhere have been identified and a programme of intervention planned, it is important that key school staff together with parents remain central to any programme of intervention. This does not diminish the role of professionals such as

EWOs, EPs, psychiatrists and specialist (CAMH) workers and others in devising and supporting the implementation of programmes, however, school staff and parents both have important and ongoing roles to play in developing programmes of intervention, implementing these, problem solving and ensuring momentum is maintained.

It is important to note that while in most mild to moderate cases of SR return to school usually results in improvement of most of the associated problems, in some cases a return to school or improved attendance in itself may not resolve the difficulties underlying the SR. In such cases, once the child or young person who is experiencing SR is supported to improve his or her attendance further intervention may be necessary to address underlying needs and help maintain the improvements. For example, a child with severe separation anxiety and other family issues may need interventions in their own right.

School-based interventions

Peer support strategies

Some school refusers experience isolation or have anxieties over friendships especially at times of transition, and a number of approaches can be used to support them. The use of peer mentoring or buddy systems can be helpful.

- Buddy systems usually involve matching the child with a peer who has volunteered to act as a supportive friend.

- Peer mentoring involves volunteers, who are often older pupils who have received some level of training in listening skills and problem solving approaches.

- Circle of Friends is an approach whereby a support network is developed. This approach is useful for improving emotional literacy and social interaction and can be formed around an identified child who is experiencing emotional, behavioural or social difficulties, or may operate without a specific focus child.

Adult mentoring

Some children with SR require increased levels of adult support to negotiate the demands of school life. On such occasions the establishment of an ongoing, supportive relationship with a member of the school staff can make a significant difference. This role might be undertaken by the nominated school key worker as described below. Opportunities for regular contact, not always focused on SR, and associated problems should be provided.

Curriculum / timetabling adjustments

Some children with SR experience anxieties around particular curriculum subjects, classroom demands or even specific teachers. Strategies used to alleviate these difficulties include providing the child with a reduced timetable, where he or she is exempted, often on a temporary basis, from lessons and or demands of teachers who are associated with increased anxiety. It may be appropriate for some of these adjustments to become permanent, while on other occasions there may be a case for discussing the needs and fears of the child with the teacher in question so that changes in the way lessons are managed and the type of demands placed on the child may be made. Other interventions may aim to provide suitable options for lunchtime and breaktime activities and locations for pupils who prefer a quiet supervised setting. On some occasions adjustments to the school timetable or curriculum may need to be accompanied by behavioural interventions, for example, relaxation training or systematic desensitisation.

Role responsibilities

Nominated lead on school refusal

As discussed in Appendix I, the literature pertaining to SR emanates mainly from the professions of psychiatry and psychology, with education sources being notable if not by their absence then by their limited presence. This is interesting in that when one considers the difficulties associated with SR which manifest around school attendance one would assume that initial interventions would usually be devised and implemented by educational professionals and parents. One possible explanation for this imbalance may be the fact that although there is a national emphasis on improving school attendance there is no requirement for schools or local authorities to identify school refusers as a specific group of non-attenders. A further barrier for education-based staff may lie in the way SR is conceptualised. As SR is often positioned as an emotional or mental health difficulty this may lead many education professionals and others to consider this area to be beyond the boundaries of their competence. While this perceived lack of specialist knowledge may be understandable it fails to acknowledge the central role parents and carers, school staff and other education professionals can play in promoting emotional wellbeing and mental health in and in supporting children and young people with SR.

It may be advantageous for schools to identify a named member of staff who will take lead responsibility for SR. This person would attend training events, keep abreast of developments in local authority strategic planning for SR and take responsibility for disseminating information to his or her colleagues in school. It may be appropriate to distinguish between this role and that of nominated key worker for individual cases of SR, although as the number of school refusers in a school at any time is likely to be few it may, in many instances be efficient, for these roles to fall to the same individual. There will be occasions when this is not desirable or practical because of capacity issues or where the nature of established relationships suggests this would be inappropriate. The school key worker role can be demanding and time consuming, especially in the early stages of establishing a programme of intervention and involves contributing to interventions and supporting the child and parents and attending multi-agency meetings. Below we consider the role of the nominated school key worker in some detail.

School key worker

An influential (not necessarily senior) member of the school staff should be nominated to contribute to multi-agency planning and reviews in relation to the child or young person – this is the school key worker. Inevitably a number of professionals and agencies become involved with this category of children such as SENCo, school health advisors, EWOs, EPs, CAMHS workers and social workers. The professional network of a typical school refusing child is shown in Figure 7.3. The role of the school key worker will involve attendance at meetings and liaison with parents and representatives from other agencies and has a time cost. However, these vulnerable pupils often require this level of investment.

Although the child or young person may receive direct involvement from specialist CAMHS or other services this is different in nature and frequency to what can be offered in school by the school key worker, in order to support the establishment of regular attendance and the implementation of the agreed programme of intervention. The establishment

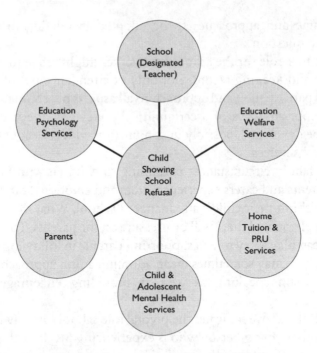

Figure 7.3 Network showing some of the professional groups that may be involved with a child or young person with school refusal

of a supportive and at times appropriately challenging relationship characterised by the Rogerian core conditions of genuineness, unconditional positive regard and empathy may be helpful. It is probably inevitable that difficulties will occur which may threaten the success of the programme of intervention; the school key worker will have a role in addressing these at the appropriate level. This might involve tackling fears or incidents relating to peer interaction. For example, bullying and feelings of isolation are often reported as being problems for children and young people who experience SR. Troubleshooting potential hazards will be a key feature of this role.

A common barrier faced by some children and young people relates to the reception they receive on their return to school following a period of absence. This can range from sarcasm to public demands for explanations and sometimes unreasonable academic demands being placed on them, any of which might threaten the success of the intervention. There is clearly a need for the school key worker to inform teachers and other key staff about the nature of SR and the aims of the intervention programme and approaches to be adopted in relating to the young person in question.

A further role for the school key worker might relate to monitoring progress and keeping records not only of attendance but of the young person's participation and approach to all aspects of school life. Creative and appropriate ways of ascertaining the views of the young person should be developed, possibly in conjunction with colleagues from psychological services.

The family circumstances pertaining to children with SR vary, but often parents and carers experience strain and emotional turmoil around re-establishing their child's attendance at school. Whatever the strategy being implemented there will be pressure on the parents. The school key worker can play a key role in supporting parents in following the agreed strategy. This may sometimes mean adopting a firm approach characterised by plain speaking as well as providing encouragement and reassurance.

All of the above indicates the pivotal role school can play in supporting a child or young person who is experiencing SR. In reality, once the programme of intervention and time frames have been agreed in a multi-agency context and systems in school set in place and relevant school colleagues briefed, the time commitment from the school key worker should be manageable. The role of the school key worker as described above is not that of expert and should not be confused with therapist, psychiatrist or any other specialist professional role. The emphasis should be on multi-agency collaboration, planning and review and the involvement of the young person and his or her parents.

Whole-school protective factors

Schools operate within a complex and at times conflicting national policy context which requires them to raise standards and continually improve their performance, to improve behaviour and attendance, promote healthy lifestyles, include children with special educational needs, and to safeguard children, to name only a few current policy imperatives! These competing requirements mean resources, both human and financial, are pulled in many different directions and there is a danger that the needs of vulnerable minority groups like school refusers may be overlooked. Factors relating to school ethos, organisational culture and policy play key roles in militating against this.

So far this chapter has focused on ways in which school staff can play a vital role in identifying and intervening early to support individual young people at risk of SR. However, there may be ways in which the ethos and organisation of schools can help prevent SR and other mental health difficulties. The government Green Paper *Every Child Matters: Change for Children* (DfES 2003) identifies the following five outcomes to be achieved by all children:

- to be healthy

- to stay safe

- to enjoy and achieve

- to make a positive contribution

- to achieve economic wellbeing.

If schools are organised to ensure that all pupils achieve the *Every Child Matters* five outcomes then they will develop structures, policies and practices which cater for all aspects of development including, emotional, social, behavioural, health and academic, in other words, they will aim to promote the wellbeing of person as a whole. Similarly, the Mental Health Foundation (1999) identifies the following school characteristics as key to the promotion of mental wellbeing in pupils:

- a committed senior management team, creating a culture within the school in which the importance of trust, integrity, democracy, equality of opportunity, and each child being valued regardless of their ability is seen as being vital

- a culture within the school which values teachers, lunchtime supervisors, and all those engaged in the care and supervision of children

- clear policies on vital issues such as behaviour and bullying; whole school behaviour policies which set out the range of acceptable behaviour for children

- high professional standards (efficient planning, marking and punctuality)

- proactive work with parents.

Becoming a 'mentally healthy school' (Figure 7.4) is an ongoing process requiring commitment and continual review and development, indeed it is an area of functioning that the Office for Standards in Education (OFSTED) requires schools to interrogate through the self-evaluation process that is now part of inspection procedures.

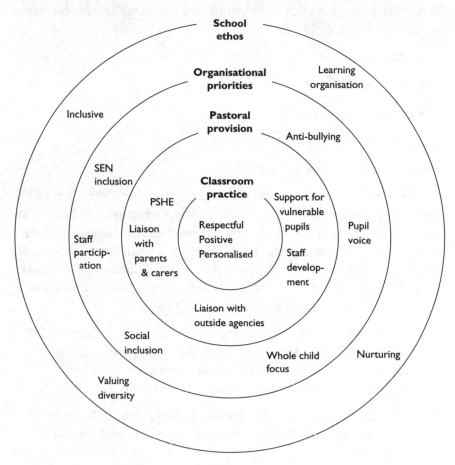

Figure 7.4 Framework for promoting mental health in schools, illustrating the need to develop a whole-school approach of positive mental health (adapted from Atkinson and Hornby 2002). This requires schools to have a clear set of policies and procedures to address mental health issues including school refusal

To support the argument that the development of a whole-school ethos promoting positive mental health will be of benefit to young people at risk of SR let us look briefly at some of the findings from the study by

Archer and colleagues (2003). As mentioned earlier this study comprised a survey of teachers and LEA personnel regarding SR, followed by more in-depth interviews. The study identified the following school-based factors as precipitating school refusal:

- the size and layout of the school, with pupils being seen as anxious about moving around the school, coping with long crowded corridors, etc.

- the structure of the school day, with pupils being seen as being anxious about unstructured times

- conflicts with teachers, pupils seen as being troubled by a particular teacher or teaching style

- transition periods, for example, when pupils move from primary to secondary school

- fear of specific subjects, particularly PE, which involves getting changed in communal areas

- academic pressures, pupils may be struggling with aspects of work

- bullying or perceived bullying

- friendship problems

- inappropriate provision, 'the wrong child in the wrong school'

- the knock-on effect of repeated absence.

This is an interesting list suggesting that a broad range of factors can affect young people at risk of SR and influence school attendance. These factors can relate to physical and structural features of the school building, to specific school routines, lessons or times of day and to relationship issues. This confirms the need for the development and implementation of whole-school policies and practices to enhance the wellbeing and inclusion of all vulnerable young people. Developing a mentally healthy school will not extinguish the vulnerabilities experienced by some young people which lead them to be at risk of school refusal, but will provide an environment that enables the identification and implementation of supportive and preventative measures and which is of benefit to the whole school community.

The case of Ben, continued

Mrs Leahy reassured Ben and his parents that if Ben encountered difficulties during class time he would be found a safe area in the library where he could take time off to cool down. All his teachers were to be informed about the plan. He was provided with an 'excuse card' to show the teachers when he felt overwhelmed. He was permitted to use it once a day.

During form periods Mrs Saunders had noticed that Ben did not appear to have any real friends but tended to associate rather loosely with Tom and Mohammed, two boys who would allow him to tag along with them from time to time. She decided to explore friendship issues with Ben during one of their meetings and found that he was frequently alone at break and lunchtimes and that this created additional anxieties for him. With Ben's agreement she approached Jermaine, another boy in the form, to be a 'buddy' for Ben. Jermaine was pleased to be asked and responded well to this role, inviting Ben to sit with him at lunchtimes and to join in some of his games.

Summary points

- School factors contribute to SR behaviour as do individual child and family characteristics.

- For a child at risk of SR, school contributes a combination of risk and protective factors which interact with individual child and family characteristics to increase or decrease the likelihood of SR behaviour developing.

- Careful analysis of risk and protective factors is a key step in intervention planning.

- Nominated school staff have important roles to play in terms of acquiring and disseminating knowledge about SR and local arrangements for supporting children with SR. In individual cases there is also a role which involves supporting the child with SR and his or her family and ensuring the planned programme of intervention is implemented in school.

- Whole-school policies which promote inclusion and emotional wellbeing of pupils can help create an ethos which can make a positive difference to children vulnerable to SR.

8 Role of Home Tuition and Pupil Referral Units

As discussed previously, schools and parents should be encouraged and supported to try a range of strategies to address SR. If tackled early enough, the indications are that mainstream schooling can continue with minimum disruption or intervention by outside agencies. However, in the most extreme cases of SR, particularly where absence has been prolonged, support strategies provided by the school alone may remain ineffective. For some school refusers, the very thought of walking through the school gate can bring about extreme fear and anxiety. For many, the length of time spent away from school avoiding the anxiety has compounded the problem to such a degree that a return to school seems totally untenable. Some pupils may say that they will never return to school in the future, such is the intensity of their feelings towards school at the time of referral and diagnosis. In this chapter we discuss the role of pupil referral units and home tuition services, with particular reference to those children and young people who exhibit extreme SR and when immediate return to school is not an option.

What is the duty of the local authority? The Education Act 2000 states that 'it is the duty of every Local Authority to make arrangements for the provision of suitable full-time or part-time education otherwise than at school for pupils of compulsory school age who, for reasons of illness, may not for any period receive suitable education unless such arrangements are made for them'. There is also a duty to provide for specific young people aged 16–19 (DfES 2000). Pupils with medical needs may be defined as:

- pupils who are physically ill, injured or recovering from medical interventions

- pupils with mental health issues

- pregnant schoolgirls who are unable to access education in their registered school.

The understanding and nature of provision of 'suitable education otherwise than at school' (EOTAS) varies between local authorities throughout England. Many local authorities provide hospital tuition as well as home tuition for pupils who cannot attend school for reasons of illness. However, there are few local authorities whose provision includes a pupil referral unit (PRU) designated solely for vulnerable pupils with medical needs. Such provision can provide a continuity of specialist education and a stable learning environment for the most vulnerable pupils who, for emotional, psychological or a variety of medical reasons, are unable to access mainstream or special school provision.

In the case of physical illness, many pupils make a full recovery within a definable time period and return to school with a minimal amount of support from external agencies. Home tuition may be provided for such pupils until they are ready for reintegration to mainstream. Physical illness or injury is often easily detected and quickly reported by families, schools and the health services, which usually results in a pupil making a speedy recovery once treated. A return to school may provide no real issues for the pupil except perhaps to ensure accessibility and that health and safety is not compromised by a return to the school site.

Mental and emotional health issues may often be less apparent to the observer and slower to be reported than physical illness or injury. For some there remains a stigma associated with mental health issues, which they would rather not be confronted with. This may be one of the key reasons why pupils experiencing mental or emotional health issues may not be reported promptly to health professionals.

Jane

Jane experienced a psychotic episode, which prevented attendance at school for some weeks. Although suitable treatment and care was provided by CAMHS, the parents would not accept the fact that Jane had a mental health issue. Her father informed the school that Jane was suffering from a viral infection as the family were unable to deal with the real issue – they believed that Jane and the whole family would be stigmatised for life. It took considerable effort and time for the family to

come to terms with the reality of the problem and make necessary
adjustment for Jane's educational needs.

The failure of some families and schools to acknowledge and support
children's mental health issues in the same way they might a physical
illness often only serves to compound the problem.

The principles and organisation of home tuition services

Many local authorities will only provide home tuition if the pupil has a
long-term or recurring medical condition, which results in missing at
least 15 days of school. Medical evidence is sought on a regular basis to
ensure that home tuition remains the most appropriate form of provision.
Referrals are usually made by schools or health professionals and are
accompanied by supporting medical evidence indicating a need for
home tuition. Medical evidence is usually provided by an appropriate
medical practitioner who may be a consultant within CAMHS, community paediatrician or hospital consultant. GPs cannot authorise requests
for home tuition.

Statutory guidance from the Department for Education and Skills
(DfES 2002) suggests that each child's minimum entitlement for home
tuition is five hours per work, however, there may be some flexibility
when taking into account any medical condition. Home tuition aims to
help pupils to keep up with their learning and return to school once
declared medically fit. It cannot act as a substitute for mainstream education. Schools remain responsible for the education and care of all of their
pupils. Some of the best examples of good practice can be seen where the
school liaises closely with the home tutor and family, working collabor-
atively to ensure that each child receives the best possible provision while
unable to attend school.

When pupils are referred for home tuition or a hospital teaching
service, it is usual for evidence to be gathered to support the provision of
EOTAS. In particular, most local authorities will wish to establish
whether pupils are able to continue to receive some or all of their education at school. This may apply particularly to pupils with mental health
needs, in which case the collaboration and support of colleagues in
CAMHS will be sought. In isolation, home tuition does not in itself
support a programme of reintegration nor can it give the child sufficient
confidence to ensure a successful return to school. Best practice shows
that the provision of timely, effective home tuition may support pupils in

avoiding long-term SR and minimise the impact of disruption to education, by:

- ensuring close liaison with the school to assist in the drawing up and implementation of an individual action plan (IAP) to ensure continuity of provision

- overseeing the delivery of work schools provide in all aspects of the curriculum to ensure that sick children are not placed at a disadvantage by their illness

- providing pupils with access to additional teaching and learning resources through, for example, curriculum online, virtual learning environments or the school's intranet

- developing strategies to raise levels of achievement for sick children by liaising with outside agencies, schools and families

- supporting pupils' reintegration to school following a period of ill health.

In the case of SR, referrals for home tuition are generally to be discouraged unless the refusal is compounded by another medical issue, which physically prevents a child from leaving the home. Home tuition can simply serve to compound the vicious cycle of increasing anxiety and can serve to support the pupil's strategies for school avoidance. Chapter 2 dealt with understanding and identifying SR, drawing attention to the fact that prolonged school absence creates further complications in itself. Home tuition can to a degree assist with addressing the fact that a school refuser has fallen behind with school work. However, most local authorities provide the recommended minimum of five hours per week, which is no substitute for full-time provision.

The other key complications and secondary handicaps, described in Chapter 2, include loss of routine, loss of friends and peer contact, resulting in isolation, and worsening of anxiety due to avoidance of the feared situation. The provision of home tuition will not address any of these complications. In fact, there are lessons to be learnt from previous cases where home tuition has been provided for SR, as shown by the following case:

Julie

Julie was a Year 9 pupil who had been absent from school for six months. Julie's mother provided notes to the school each time Julie complained of feeling unwell, which became more frequent as time went on. The reasons for absence included stomach upsets and headaches. Eventually, Julie refused to go to school completely and her mother was faced each morning with crying and shouts of, 'You hate me. I can't go to school if I'm not well.'

Following the involvement of the EWS, Julie was referred to her GP and ultimately to CAMHS. She was also referred to the local authority for home tuition, which she received for five hours per week over a three-month period. During this time Julie was able to address some of the issues with her school work and catch up in some subjects. However, the home tutor observed that Julie was becoming increasingly withdrawn from the outside world, retreating into a routine revolving around the cocoon she had made for herself at home. Julie became increasingly anxious about leaving the house and would only get dressed on days when the home tutor was due at the family home.

Rather than being helpful, home tuition can serve to compound the problems of SR. In cases like Julie's lessons should be learnt and good practice should involve supporting the pupil back to school rather than bringing schooling to the pupil's home. By receiving tuition, Julie saw even less reason to attend school. The issues Julie faced were not primarily caused by or associated with her academic studies. She had become emotionally distressed about attending school, which had ultimately resulted in complete social isolation, extreme anxiety and severe social disability (see Figure 2.2, The vicious cycle in school refusal).

In understanding cases like Julie's, an awareness of the nature of anxiety is essential (see Chapter 3). For Julie, the provision of home tuition negatively reinforced her avoidance of the feared situation by removing the need to attend school completely. As long as the home tuition continued, Julie believed she would not have to face school. However well meaning, the decision to provide home tuition meant that Julie would never be in a position to confront and 'get used' to her anxiety (habituation) and come to terms with it. This resulted in an avoidance–reinforcement cycle that very quickly became self-perpetuating. With the agreement of CAMHS, home tuition was withdrawn.

Julie, continued

Julie deteriorated rapidly and refused to leave her home. She locked herself in the bathroom if visitors attempted to talk to her. Her behaviour began to dominate the whole family and her mother felt guilty if any confrontation with Julie resulted in tears and shouting. The anxiety and aggressive defensiveness became such a problem for Julie that she was prescribed medication by CAMHS. In lengthy discussions with CAMHS, the home tuition ceased; it was important to remove one of the factors reinforcing Julie's avoidance cycle.

Over a three-month period, Julie became calmer and more amenable to her family. She was able to leave the home, albeit late at night, when she felt nobody would see her. Julie's progress was monitored weekly through meetings with her mother and CAMHS. After three months, through collaborative working between CAMHS, the home tuition service and the EWS, it was decided that the home tutor should re-establish contact with Julie, but not to discuss school work. The home tutor subsequently visited Julie and spoke to her in a 'mentoring' capacity. It was made clear to Julie that she could not continue to receive home tuition as this would not help her to progress further. Conversations focused on planning for her future, breaking any plans down into manageable chunks and reassuring her that there would be a good deal of support in helping Julie to face her anxieties about school. An alternative solution was proposed to Julie; to attend a local PRU for pupils with medical needs who were in a similar situation. The thought of starting somewhere afresh, with unknown routines and faces, filled Julie with more anxiety than facing up to those fears she already experienced about her existing school.

Close liaison between all parties followed, with the school resuming a lead role, and Julie attended school for the first time in over nine months. School support was crucial, from agreeing a timescale for reintegration to ensuring that a friend would be allowed to sit with Julie for as long as she felt she needed this.

The principles and organisation of pupil referral units

As stated earlier, the nature of provision of EOTAS varies between local authorities. There are few local authorities whose provision does not include a PRU designated solely for vulnerable pupils with medical needs. Such provision can provide a continuity of specialist education and a stable learning environment for the most vulnerable pupils who for emotional, psychological or a variety of medical reasons, are unable to access mainstream or special school provision.

Where PRU provision exists for vulnerable pupils with medical needs, local authorities will have their own referral and admission criteria. Generally speaking, referrals to a PRU can be made by a variety of professionals, including school teachers whose designated responsibility is the care of pupils with medical issues; health professionals, including CAMHS and educational psychologists and also the EWS. What is clear is that collaborative working and effective communication between interested parties ensures appropriate provision and pathways for individual pupils.

With specific reference to SR, referrals to PRUs might range from pupils with anxiety who feel traumatised by the thought of school to pupils with other mental health problems (e.g. severe obsessive compulsive disorder; OCD), resulting in total self-imposed social exclusion. For extreme cases of SR a PRU may provide a more palatable option, bridging the gap between school and the social isolation of staying at home. Often this is more realistic and acceptable to the young person than returning immediately to a large school. Attendance at a PRU can provide the school refuser with a positive experience of education and allow them to restore routine to their lives.

Effective provision in a unit providing a calm and positive ethos may include the development of social skills to enhance self-esteem. Good practice in PRUs involves working closely with the multidisciplinary team to address the individual's problems. Support and advice will be offered to parents and schools through regular reviews of pupil progress. Ultimately PRUs should be able to facilitate successful reintegration to mainstream schools. Any pupil receiving support from a PRU should be made aware that their ultimate goal will be to return to school as soon as their health permits them to do so. Pupils and families should understand that a return to school can assist in the successful ongoing treatment of some of the anxieties compounded by absence.

Common practice involves the provision of a suitable programme for integration to the PRU, which requires the complete and resolute support of parents or carers. If the vicious cycle of SR is to be broken, parents and carers need to understand that they are part of the solution also. By the time SR has been identified, many parents have become overinvolved in the process leading to the problem. Many feel helpless and can only deal with the situation by complying with their child's wishes not to attend school; for some it becomes upsetting to challenge the school refuser and this in itself must be addressed. Many PRUs find that time invested with parents pays dividends also. Parents sometimes need to be reminded to pay attention to and reward positive behaviour and ignore the negative. In the case of SR, ignoring the negative might mean agreeing to ignore minor physical complaints that have no medical basis. It is clear that PRUs cannot work without the full support of parents and carers in trying to overcome SR.

Effective PRUs tend to provide a balanced curriculum, combining an academic diet with social and emotional skill building. Generally speaking, the role of the PRU will be at least three dimensional:

- to address the damaging effects of isolation

- to provide a curriculum which balances the academic with social skills

- to build emotional defences through confidence building to enable pupils to return smoothly to mainstream school.

An example of the work done at PRUs is changing thought and language patterns in pupils showing severe SR. Pupils are encouraged to understand and believe that things can and will be different for them in the future; that change is possible. Work is undertaken with small groups of school refusers to build and reinforce positive expectations and pupils learn how to deal with negative feelings such as humiliation and failure. Pupils may be assigned a peer buddy who can help the more socially anxious pupils to feel at ease. Often the buddies are themselves working at ways of addressing their own issues with SR, which can have a mutual benefit: buddies gain confidence themselves through working with their peers.

As discussed in Appendix I, research findings are unclear, but there is some evidence to suggest that behavioural approaches to dealing with SR tend to enjoy more success than other forms of treatment. Within the safety of a PRU environment, pupils can undertake behavioural programmes which are based on the principle of systemic desensitisation through graded exposure. Exposure-based interventions might include a range of strategies, from meeting a trusted teacher from school to making a brief, informal visit to the school site, escorted by a trusted member of staff from the PRU. Work is undertaken with pupils to correct the thinking patterns and beliefs held about school, which contribute towards anxiety and ultimately, SR.

John

One Year 8 pupil, John, experienced a severe bout of anxiety at the time of attending school (he was known to have difficulties in attending school for some time) so much so that he was found to be disoriented and confused. It resulted in hospitalisation in the local paediatric ward for a period of time. CAMHS were involved in his care and treatment and a prompt referral to a PRU was made. Through partnership and close collaboration, including information sharing, John's needs were identified early and a programme for addressing his subsequent SR put in place. On his first day, John arrived at the PRU in tears and he was begging his mother not to leave him. Following the advice she was given during the initial planning meeting, John's mother withdrew and showed no emotion at leaving John. She offered him a few positive words and reassured him that she would collect him later. Within a short period of time, of perhaps 20 minutes or so, the learning mentor had placed John at ease, offering reassurance and praise for attending the centre.

John was assigned to an older peer buddy and by the lunch break he was running around with his peer buddy and another pupil playing games outside. Within a few days of attending the centre, the growth in his self-confidence and esteem was noted by all staff. John was quickly acclimatised to being in a routine and work on developing and reinforcing a positive attitude and changing his negative beliefs was successful. John was also taught a range of coping strategies, which involved confronting, rather than avoiding, his fears.

SR is an eminently treatable problem if it is reported swiftly and dealt with appropriately by the family, school and relevant agencies, including CAMHS. The work of the PRU is made much more difficult as cases go undetected or inappropriately reported. Any delay in diagnosing SR and ruling out other medical issues can be detrimental to the success of reha-bilitation; often resulting in extreme SR. Within the PRU, school refusers are systematically taught to confront, rather than avoid, their fears. The presence of a small but similar-minded group provides safety for the school refuser in trying out new skills and practising dealing with situations and people they previously avoided. Pupils learn a range of coping strategies, including being able to think through a threatening situation and be realistic and positive in their thoughts. School refusers can learn to deal with situations which they had previously found threatening. Social skills are rebuilt and there is a heavy emphasis on improving personal and interpersonal skills. As social skills show signs of improvement, isolation usually decreases. Participation in a variety of previously avoided activities begins to increase, including social activity, as well as academic interest.

Rehabilitation to mainstream school

When a pupil is ready for reintegration to mainstream school all interested parties should understand their support roles. A supported, well-planned return to school is likely to be most successful in the long term.

John, continued

When the time came for John's reintegration to mainstream school he played a key role in the planning process. John's parents, CAMHS and key teaching staff were all committed to ensuring that John's reintegration was to be successful. John's views were taken into account regarding his timetable, which was adjusted slightly to accommodate his wishes and ensure he succeeded. John was provided with a reintegration programme (Return to School Plan) and he identified a key worker within the school, with whom he felt comfortable enough to talk through any problem if it should arise.

Following the planning meeting and within just one month of attending the PRU, John had attended his mainstream school for his first informal visit. This was followed by subsequent visits, providing opportunities to meet staff, peers named by John and opportunities to sit in lessons with some support from the PRU's learning mentor. When the time came for John to attend more fully, he attended school each morning and the PRU each afternoon. Following a review of how things were going, John was given a 'safety net', at his own request, which he had not used even some three months after reintegration! This included, having a pass to leave lessons *should he feel the need to do so* and having access to a quiet area or office with the mutual agreement of the school. However, the knowledge that John had the safety net reinforced his confidence at school.

For some long-term school refusers and their families, any contact with school may become less frequent as time progresses. It is essential that the school continues to play a part in the child's life and efforts are made for the child and family to still feel that they are part of the school. With home tuition, depending on the relationship the school has with the family and the child, this may include home visits by a familiar member of staff, sending work home regularly and arranging for its collection. Where a child attends a PRU, the school should remain closely involved, with the PRU acting as intermediary between home and school. In addition, schools should be encouraged to send communication home regularly, including letters to parents and newsletters. Some schools may have a learning mentor or another member of staff who is well placed to make good links with the family and the child. This should be encouraged in the early days of SR and built upon until such a time as the pupil is ready to return to school in any capacity, to ensure successful reintegration.

The key to successful reintegration is partnership between the family, school and other involved agencies. The provision of education to pupils with medical needs, including school refusers, whether through home tuition, hospital teaching or PRU, aims to maintain pupil progress in all aspects of their rehabilitation. This is essential to the timely and successful reintegration into school of each pupil in accordance with individual needs.

Summary points
Pupil referral units

- PRUs can provide a continuity of specialist education and a stable learning environment for the most vulnerable pupils who for emotional, psychological or a variety of medical reasons, are unable to access mainstream or special school provision.

- PRUs may provide a more palatable option for school refusers, bridging the gap between school and the social isolation of remaining at home.

- If the vicious cycle of SR is to be broken, parents and carers need to understand that they are also part of the solution.

- Behavioural approaches to dealing with SR tend to enjoy more success than other forms of treatment. Within the safety of a

PRU environment pupils can undertake behavioural programmes which are based on the principle of systemic desensitisation through graded exposure.

Home tuition

- Home tuition should not be provided routinely for school refusers unless there are additional medical reasons preventing the child from leaving the home.

- Home tuition can prevent pupils from confronting anxieties and overcoming them (habituation).

- Home tuition can compound the vicious cycle of increasing anxiety and can serve to support the pupil's strategies for school avoidance, reinforcing the avoidance cycle.

- Home/school support should be used effectively as a tool to re-establish links and negotiations with school where absence has been prolonged. This *may* fall into the remit of the home tuition service if there is already involvement. This should be carefully planned so that the avoidance cycle is not reinforced.

9 Strategic Planning

Throughout this book so far the importance of multi-agency involvement in assessing and intervening to find solutions to SR has been emphasised. 'Multi-agency working' seems to be the mantra for children's services at the present time, as it is enshrined in the Children Act 2004 which among other things places a duty on local authorities and their partner agencies 'to promote cooperation between agencies in order to improve children's well-being'. Professionals from all agencies are beginning to ask themselves what effective multi-agency or collaborative work looks like. This is an important question when attempting to plan at a strategic level for the needs of vulnerable groups of pupils such as school refusers. Furthermore, the very nature of SR with its dimensions of mental health concerns, family-based factors, school factors, peer relationship factors, etc. demands multi-agency collaboration for strategic planning. For our purposes strategic planning refers to taking a long- or medium-term perspective and adopting a focus beyond that of the individual child.

One of the challenges to effective multi-agency work relates to communication; how can we ensure that professionals have a shared understanding of the issue they are addressing, in this case SR. Each professional group will have its own terminology, philosophy, priorities and ways of delivering services. For example, EWOs and school staff may experience a pressure to improve attendance and ensure this is recorded appropriately, there may be an inclination to seek medical opinion; educational psychologists may be inclined to adopt a systemic perspective, looking at school and family related factors impacting on the young person; GPs and school health advisors may seek a psychiatric opinion and psychiatrists may experience a pressure to address family and within child factors. These may be stereotypical assumptions as to how different professionals will respond to SR but serve to illustrate the diverse perspectives that need to be considered in developing a strategic approach. Consequently the development of an agreed working definition of SR will be necessary. This would be facilitated through the formation of a group of individuals representing key professional groups, with the task of developing strategy.

To be effective, the strategic group cannot be divorced from the realities of practice and so the process of strategy development might best be characterised as involving two-way communication between the different professional groups and strategic group members. Parent perspectives and child/young person views will form a necessary and key dimension of strategic planning.

In this chapter we aim to identify key principles for strategic planning to address the needs of children and young people with SR and their families. We are aware of the pitfalls in offering prescriptive advice in relation to this complex, heterogeneous group.

Agreeing a local working definition of school refusal

As discussed earlier there is no one absolute definition of SR. It is a complex area that is still being researched. Agreeing a working definition will involve discussion, reference to research and policy documentation and perhaps liaison with local authorities or services. A working definition is just that, and will be open to appropriate review. Agreeing a working definition of SR is likely to involve exploring how a practitioner would set about deciding whether SR might be a possibility; in other words what information would be required to rule out other forms of SNA.

Evidence-based planning

Strategic planning can be greatly disadvantaged by a lack of real knowledge, consequently the relationship between strategists and practitioners is vital. It is important not to make assumptions about working practices but to review or 'research' in a fairly objective way what currently happens. Such a review should address problems or gaps in the system or systems currently employed. This can be a challenging exercise because professional groups or even individuals may be open to criticism. It is important to adopt a sensitive approach which avoids personalisation of issues and scapegoating.

Strategic developments as part of CAMHS strategy

Child and adolescent mental health services are designed to

> promote the mental health and psychological wellbeing of children and young people, and provide high quality, multidisciplinary mental health services to all children and young people with mental health problems and disorders to ensure effective assessment, treatment and support, for them and their families. (Every Child Matters 2003)

This description of CAMHS relates directly to the group of young people we are concerned with. It should be noted that the term CAMHS can be used in two different ways, one referring to specialist services such as those delivered by clinical psychologists, family therapists and child and adolescent psychiatrists, the other referring to non-specialist services whose primary function is not mental health. CAMHS services are delivered through a four-tier system with the majority of mental health difficulties being dealt with at tiers 1 and 2.

> Tier 1: CAMHS is provided by practitioners who are not mental health specialists such as school staff, youth workers, education welfare officers and school health advisors.

> Tier 2: CAMHS is provided by specialists working in community and primary care settings, often working as single agencies such as GPs, educational psychologists and school health advisors.

> Tier 3: CAMHS is provided by individual specialist mental health workers; frequently, they will be members of multidisciplinary child and adolescent teams; they often deal with more complex difficulties. At this level, specialist staff work as individual professionals.

> Tier 4: CAMHS is provided through highly specialised outpatient teams and in-patient facilities for children and young people with the most serious problems.

Strategic planning in relation to children and young people with SR must occur within the CAMHS framework as outlined above. It is important that the practitioners represented are aware of their role in the promotion of the mental health and wellbeing of their clients. This does not mean that intervention will take place in a phased manner with the young person moving up through the tiers. Some young people with SR will require involvement from practitioners from more than one tier, indeed the model of multi-agency planning discussed in earlier chapters with the school remaining central to the process would necessitate this type of involvement.

An important question to address in terms of strategic planning for SR is when and how to involve specialist CAMHS services; too early an involvement can result in unnecessary medicalisation of the young person's needs, which may act to inhibit the active involvement of non-specialist services. On the other hand, delays in seeking specialist involvement from CAMHS can lead to the young person being absent from school for prolonged periods and an increase in worrying behaviours. There can be no hard and fast rule about when to involve specialist CAMHS services and each case must be considered on its merits; however, it is likely that early identification and intervention, before patterns of SNA become established would be conducted appropriately by non-specialist CAMHS services at Tiers 1 and 2.

A further consideration relates to the delineation of roles of the different professionals who may become involved in supporting young people with SR. As above there are no prescribed roles to be adopted that lead inevitably to successful outcomes and there must be room for the network of professionals working with the young person and his family to formulate their approach and negotiate their roles based on the specifics of the case, however, agreements or guidelines about broad service roles and responsibilities might be usefully pursued.

Early intervention

Early intervention refers to the drive towards intervening at the earliest opportunity to support young people and their families before the problems of SR become entrenched and when the child is younger rather than older. The desirability of this is obvious, long-standing patterns of SNA, anxiety and avoidant behaviour, and parental acceptance or collusion can become intransigent. However, policies promoting early intervention have implications for monitoring of attendance and patterns of absence, this in turn requires training for attendance officers or other staff in schools responsible for attendance matters. The dissemination of information about SR is a necessary aspect of strategic planning. A lack of knowledge about SR will mean school staff and others who have direct contact with young people and their families are unable to recognise early signs and consult with practitioners to secure appropriate help. It may be worthwhile considering developing a specific framework or checklist to support professionals in identifying and planning interventions for school refusers.

Schools as central to identification and intervention

As stated above, school staff have an essential part to play in the early identification of attendance and emotional concerns which may signal SR, however, their role does not stop there. For interventions to be effective it is important that school staff are central to planning them and in monitoring progress. The school as an institution may present problems for the young person with SR but conversely it is also pivotal to the development of solutions. Systems whereby young people with SR are identified, then referred to agencies external to the school in linear progression, with specialist CAMHS services being positioned as the ultimate referral point are often time consuming, ineffective, repetitive and disempowering. The principle of schools remaining central to the process means the nominated member of school staff remains actively involved throughout the planning, intervention and review cycle. This approach is also conducive to capacity-building in schools for addressing the needs of school refusers.

The continuum of school refusal

Strategic planning needs to consider what might be termed the continuum of SR, as discussed in Chapter 2. In conceptualising SR as a continuum we are acknowledging degrees of emotional distress and difficulties with attendance; at one end of the continuum there will be children and young people who manage to maintain full attendance despite high levels of anxiety and reluctance while at the other end there are individuals who are persistent in their non-attendance at school and through this behaviour avoid what they experience to be threatening situations. Part of the continuum (the less severe end) will be catered for primarily by the school and education support services, while the more severe end will require involvement from specialist CAMHS and in some cases alternative educational provision like home tuition services or a PRU specialising in meeting the needs of children with severe attendance difficulties related to mental health concerns. Important aspects of catering for this continuum of need lie in education and training; in educating school staff, parents and the community at large about SR and mental health issues and in increasing the capacity of education services to address needs and clarifying consultation and referral routes. Access routes for specialist educational provision must be transparent, but one should not underestimate the significance of professional judgement in decision-making in individual cases.

We have stated our belief in the pivotal role communication plays in effective multi-agency work. One aspect of communication we wish to emphasise is that of consultation. Consultation does not imply referral, but rather a working together that acknowledges the expertise of each party with a focus on seeking solutions. This type of process is useful in helping to build capacity and can facilitate effective decision-making in individual cases; consequently in considering the continuum of SR strategic planning needs to address issues around access to consultation.

Collate and review information

A key task of strategic planning is to collate data on cases of SR and how they have been dealt with, which professional groups have been involved and also to consider any difficulties with agreed systems. This process provides a mechanism for planned review and adjustment to practices. The views of children and young people and their parents will make an essential contribution to a review of processes.

The case of Ben

The issue of SR in general and the case of Ben in particular was discussed in one of the staff meetings. The discussion centred on the need for flexibility and good communication among teachers. To Mrs Leahy's surprise, several teachers said that they were familiar with children and young people with problems similar to Ben's. Mrs Leahy raised Ben's case with Mr Simmons, the head teacher, and they agreed that the topic of SR could be usefully discussed at a forthcoming senior management team meeting as there had been a number of children over the years who seemed to have these sort of difficulties. An outcome of the senior management meeting was that SR would become the topic of one of the schools teacher training days and representatives from education welfare, educational psychology and CAMHS would be invited to help plan and deliver the training. When Mr Simmons approached these services he found there was a multi-agency steering group in operation whose main remit was to plan co-ordinated delivery of services for children with SR. He made arrangements for himself and Mrs Leahy to attend the next steering group meeting.

Postscript – Ben's progress

Ben's RSP started well. As agreed Ben's father took a week off to support his wife in taking Ben to school. The first day was the most difficult. Ben had the usual tummy pains and begged to be able to be at home. His mother was firm and with the help of her husband got him into school. He was received by Mrs Leahy and spent some time in the library before going into class. The programme was a success over the next two weeks. On the third week it ran into trouble. On the Monday Ben experienced severe diarrhoea and tummy pains and was unable to be taken to school by his mother. Instinctively she wanted to take him to the doctor. But she decided to phone her husband at work and check with him. He insisted that she resist any temptation to medicalise the problem and rang Mrs Leahy to appraise her of the situation. It was decided to give Ben time till afternoon and take him to school late. This arrangement worked well.

Over the next week there were two more days that he found attendance difficult. Mrs Leahy was beginning to doubt herself. She then contacted the steering group and sought their advice. It did not take her long to realise that the RSP had been too ambitious and needed to be reviewed. She convened a meeting of the family to review the RSP. Following the meeting the plan was redrawn allowing more time for full-time return to school. However, she was keen to get Ben into full-time attendance before the end of the term. Ben was making good progress. He told Mrs Saunders that he had expected to be embarrassed by his classmates asking questions about his school absence. But he was surprised to find that they asked him 'Are you better now?' He was moved by this show of concern. After all, things were not as bad as he thought. One other development which helped his integration into school was that his relationship with his classmate Jermaine was getting better. He had invited him home and the visit went well. He was feeling less isolated in school. By the end of the term Ben's attendance he had achieved almost full attendance, albeit with a few half day absences. He was coping well with the morning anxiety although it was more difficult for him after a Bank Holiday week end. Mrs Leahy and his parents anticipated problems after the term holidays and made preparations well in advance by visiting school the week before school reopened.

Summary points

- Strategic planning in relation to SR needs to involve multi-agency collaboration and might usefully be conceptualised as two-way communication between practice and strategy.

- Key principles for strategic planning include:

  ○ *agreeing a working definition of SR*

  ○ *evidence-based planning* – strategic planning should follow a careful review, involving key professional groups, of what currently happens and difficulties or gaps in the system

  ○ *strategic developments as part of CAMHS* – strategic planning needs to be cognisant of the role of specialist and non-specialist practitioners in promoting positive mental health and how this relates to SR. Issues of access to specialist CAMHS services and role definition need to be addressed

  ○ *early intervention* – this has particular implications for the way attendance is monitored in schools and underlines the importance of training staff to identify early signs of possible SR

  ○ *schools as central to identification and intervention* – the role of school staff is pivotal not only in helping to identify SR but also in planning and intervention and in monitoring progress once school attendance has been re-established. The importance of capacity building in school to cater for children with SR is an important consideration

  ○ *the continuum of SR* – strategic planning must take account of the continuum of need in relation to SR. This relates not only to CAMHS provision, specialist and non-specialist, but also the need for a range of responses in terms of educational support and provision

  ○ *collate and review information* – strategic planning is not a once and for all endeavour, so it is important to create a mechanism to review and adjust practices and systems.

Appendix I What is Known about School Refusal: Research Findings

The scientific literature on the subject of SR has developed separately and independently along two different lines. On one hand, there is a wealth of psychological literature. The number of research studies, reviews and books written on the subject from a psychological and psychiatric perspective is voluminous. For example, a search of literature using the words 'school' and 'refusal' for articles since 1980 in the databases MEDLINE, PsychoINFO, EMBASE, DN-DATA, British Nursing Index and CINAML(R) produced 261 references, all from psychological and psychiatric literature. On the other hand, the development of educational research into SR has been rather slow and patchy. The result is two rather divorced schools of thought and practice with little cross-fertilisation between them. The majority of studies carried out in child mental health settings have been carried out on selected samples, for example, with children attending child mental health clinics. These findings might therefore not be representative of mild to moderate SR more commonly seen in by educational services.

As frontline practitioners, it might be expected that teachers and educational professionals would have been the first to identify SR, understand its causes and devise strategies to manage them. Hence the lack of systematic studies from educational circles does come as a surprise. One of the main reasons for this state of affairs is that although teachers have known all along that there was a group of children with school attendance problems who were loosely called school refusers or school phobics, official SNA figures do not recognise school refusers as a separate group and they tend to be subsumed under truants or parentally condoned absences. Unfortunately, academic literature in education has followed the same line of thought.

SR is a complex subject and a number of existential difficulties face the researcher who embarks on studying it. First, as pointed out in Chapter 1, there is no universally agreed definition of SR. Second, the terminology used to describe this group of children had been inconsistent and confusing. Third, operational definition of the term school refusal is beset with difficulties. For example, how many school days have to be lost before calling it SR? Many would argue that the child with extreme reluctance to attend school due to emotional difficulties but managing to put in sufficient school attendance with great effort and cost should be included in the definition, and that absence from school is not a necessary condition for its identification. But for research one needs hard criteria. It is interesting to note that some of the studies carried out by psychiatrists have used 40 per cent school absence over a term as the cut-off points for defining this group (e.g. Bools, Foster, Brown *et al.* 1990). Many in education would consider this a criterion too remote from normal practice. The differing lenses used to view school refusers by educationalists and mental health professionals and lack of a common language to describe the phenomenon have been important barriers to our understanding of the subject.

A survey of 60 LEAs in England illustrates the complexities in the way schools and teachers understood the issues involved. This study, commissioned by the Local Government Association, looked into the perceptions of LEAs, schools and teachers about what they understood by SR and school phobia (Archer *et al.* 2003). Although it was not a study *into* SR, rather *about* it, the findings are revealing:

- Only a quarter of the LEAs routinely collected information on SR; there was great variation among them in the numbers reported.

- Out of a total of 280 schools, only 48 (17%) distinguished SR as a separate category of school non-attendance.

- Of the 48 schools only one school had written guidance on SR for school staff or parents.

- There was no clear understanding among educational practitioners as to what SR (or school phobia) was.

- In the 48 schools a total of 293 pupils were regarded as fitting the description of SR or school phobia.

- In the above schools those with primary responsibility for the group varied and were almost equally distributed between EWS, head of year, SENCo and the head teacher.

SR had received considerable attention in child mental health since its first description by Broadwin in 1932. In 1941 Johnson coined the term 'school phobia' to describe a group of children whose school absence was due to anxieties about separation from the mother (Johnson, Falstein and Szureck 1941). Influenced by psychoanalytic thinking, early studies focused on separation difficulties encountered by children and parents and these consisted mainly of case reports. The scientific study of SR was ushered by Berg and colleagues (1969) when, for the first time, they provided an operational definition that has now come to be widely accepted. These criteria include the following: severe difficulties attending school, often resulting in prolonged absence; severe emotional upset at the prospect of going to school; staying at home with parent's knowledge and absence of antisocial characteristics such as stealing, lying and destructiveness (see also Chapter 1). The term school refusal has gained universal acceptability and terms such as 'school phobia' and school avoidance are considered to be obsolete (King and Bernstein, 2001).

Prevalence

There are no accurate figures for the prevalence of SR. The difficulties in defining SR precisely have been the main problem. Even when criteria are agreed upon, the estimates can vary dramatically. For example, a well-conducted study of SR in Venezuelan school children produced a prevalence rate of 0.4 per cent. This figure was arrived at when there was agreement by teachers, parents *and* the child that the SR was due to emotional distress and fear. However, when the rates were calculated on the basis of report from one source only (either teachers or children), the prevalence was found to be 5.4 per cent (Granell de Aldaz, Vivas, Gelfand *et al.* 1984). A US study using the criteria stipulated by Berg *et al.* (1969) documented an SR rate of 0.4 per cent (Ollendick and Mayer 1984). Epidemiological studies extrapolated from referrals to clinic suggest that SR occurs in approximately 5 per cent of all school-age children (Last and Strauss 1990). A large survey of children absent from schools in a particular week in England, based on the opinion of EWOs produced a figure of 1.3 per cent for SR (National Association of Chief Education Welfare Officers 1975). The authors conclude that based on these findings there were 20,000 school refusers in England and Wales at any given time but concede that these were conservative estimates. Overall, the more widely accepted prevalence rate for SR is between 1 and 2 per cent (King, Tonge, Heyne *et al.* 1998).

There appears to be no relationship between SR and social class. Early studies reported that the level of intellectual or academic ability of school refusers were above average. More recent studies have demonstrated that the measured level of intelligence in school refusers is in the average range. A well-conducted study by Hampe, Miller, Barrett *et al.* (1973) which measured the IQs of more than 50 school refusers showed that their average full IQ was 98.9 points. Numerous other studies have confirmed this finding. Most studies suggest that SR tends to be equally common in boys and girls. SR can occur throughout the entire range of school years, but tends to peak at key transition times, i.e. at ages 5–6 (school entry), 10–11 (transfer to secondary school) and 14 (Ollendick and Mayer 1984). Across schoolgoing age the peak presentation is between 11 to 12 years. In general, older children tend to show more severe difficulties and have a poorer prognosis than younger ones (Atkinson, Quarrington and Cyr 1985).

Factors contributing to school refusal

In the literature there is general agreement that SR is the outcome of a combination of factors. The factors that predispose to it may be different from those that precipitate it and these may in turn be different from those that perpetuate it. There is general consensus that children who show SR have a behaviourally inhibited temperament. Such children have been described as shy, introverted and fearful. They are vulnerable to stress and predisposed to developing anxiety reactions.

Family stress has been found to be a significant factor contributing to the development of SR. Illness in family members, family break up and bereavements are associated with SR as is stress at school over transition from one school to another and change of class. Curiously, there is little research on the link between bullying and SR although on self-reported measures it is one of the common reasons given by school refusers for not attending school.

The family context in SR has been the focus in a number of studies. Using various family assessment measures a number of patterns of family functioning have been described. For example, Kearney and Silverman (1995) used the Family Environment Scale in families with school refusers and report identifying four family types: enmeshed family, conflictive family, isolated family and detached family. Other workers using different family assessment tools have claimed to have identified other 'dysfunctional' family interactional patterns. In the absence of normative data on family functioning (i.e. what is a 'normal' family?), these findings mean little. There is also the question of direction of causality. Does SR cause family difficulties or do family difficulties cause SR? There is, however, agreement among authorities that family is an important part of the context in which SR occurs and that for any intervention to be successful family involvement is essential (King and Bernstein 2001). Many studies and case reports have found increased rates of anxiety and depression in parents, especially mothers, of children with SR (Berg *et al.* 1981).

Few studies have investigated the specific role of school-related factors in SR. The main thrust of educational research has been in relation to truancy rather than SR (e.g. O'Keeffe and Stoll 1995). While it has been taken at face value that peer bullying, poor supervision, unfriendly teachers and a generally hostile school environment promote SR, there is very little research evidence to support these assertions. Equally, change of school is rarely effective for overcoming the problem of SR.

Diagnostic studies

SR is not a psychiatric diagnosis; rather it is a description of a constellation of behaviours. SR is a relatively common reason for referral to CAMHS. It has been estimated that 1 in 20 referrals to CAMHS is due to SR (Last and Strauss 1998). Predictably many meet the criteria for mental health disorders, especially anxiety disorders (as specified by diagnostic systems such as ICD-10 or DSM-IV). These findings from clinic populations have to be interpreted with caution because the findings are true of the referred group (who are invariably more disabled) and are not representative of the entire spectrum of SR. It should be noted that the earliest studies of school refusers were carried out by psychiatrists and psychologists on those who were admitted to child psychiatric units. These wards had teaching units attached to them and gradual introduction to the unit was considered to be part of 'rehabilitation' with eventual return to their usual school. At present it is doubtful if any child and adolescent psychiatric unit would admit school refusers.

Hence we must look to studies carried out in the community if we are to understand the prevalence of child and adolescent mental health problems in school refusers. A study by Berg, Butler, Franklin *et al.* (1993) helps to put the problem in perspective. They carried out a study of 80 youths, aged 13 to 15 years, who had not attended school (unauthorised absences) for at least 40 per cent of a school term. This study is remarkable because, unlike previous studies those examined populations referred to clinics, the sample was drawn from a normal school population. The results showed that half the sample had no psychiatric disorder, a third had a disruptive behaviour disorder and a fifth had an anxiety or mood disorder. A similar study by Bools *et al.* (1990) assessed 100 children with severe school attendance problems and found that only half met criteria for a psychiatric disorder, with truants more likely to have conduct disorder and the school refusers more likely to have anxiety disorders. A study from the US (Egger, Costello and Angold 2003) of a sample of 4500 children from 9 to 16 showed that SNA fell into three subgroups: pure truancy (5.8%), pure anxious school refusal (1.6%) and 'mixed school refusal' (0.5%). Please note that these studies included *all* school non-attenders.

There is now incontrovertible evidence from numerous studies that the prevalence of definable mental health disorders in school refusers is quite high. Of these anxiety disorders are most common. In studies that have looked specifically at clinical depression in school refusers there is no clear evidence of its increased occurrence in this population. Several diagnostic studies have examined the prevalence of various psychiatric disorders *specifically* among school refusers. The following study is typical of the research into severe school refusal. Last and Strauss (1990) examined 63 school refusing youths aged 7–17 referred to an outpatient anxiety disorder clinic. The most common primary diagnosis was separation anxiety disorder (38%), followed by social phobia (30%) and simple phobia (22%). Many children had more than one diagnosis, the most common concurrent diagnosis was generalised anxiety disorder. Recent clinical studies point to three types of anxious school refusers: those with separation anxiety, those with social phobia or simple phobia and those who have other anxieties and/or depression. Based on a review of studies over the previous ten years King and Bernstein (2001) concluded that although the SR group (as defined above) is a heterogeneous group with variable presentation, it comprises three primary diagnostic subgroups:

1. Separation-anxiety group: This was the most common disorder in school refusers and occurred more commonly in the younger age group. The mean age of onset for this group is 8–9 years. Mothers of these children had experienced SR and had a history of panic disorder or panic disorder with agoraphobia.

2. Social phobia (or simple phobia) group: This group is somewhat older and have more severe SR. Their parents were more likely to have social anxiety or phobia.

3. Other anxiety disorder group (e.g. generalised anxiety disorder) or depression: This mostly occurred in adolescents.

In summary, psychologists and psychiatrists have focused their attention on the severe end of the SR spectrum and found them to be a diagnostically heterogeneous group. Studies of children referred to CAMHS show that the younger school refusing child typically shows features of separation anxiety disorder and the older school refuser exhibits characteristics of social phobia, although generalised anxiety cases are common. These studies, based on children referred to clinics, no doubt represent the more 'severe' cases and caution needs to be exercised when extrapolating these results to 'common or garden' school refusers seen by practitioners in schools.

Assessment

The heterogeneous nature of SR and the factors that contribute to it demand that the assessment be informed by a variety of procedures involving evaluation of the child, family and the school circumstances. A number of behaviour-rating scales and self-report instruments have been developed for research purposes, but are of little use in day-to-day work with school refusers. In practice, most assessments are based on interviews with the parents, child and information from school. Moreover, the use of these rating scales has not been shown to add to usual forms of assessments. One exception to this is the School Refusal Assessment Scale devised by Kearney.

Christopher Kearney, a US psychologist, has been a prolific researcher and writer on the subject of SNA and deserves special mention. In his extensive work on school non-attendance he employs the umbrella term *school refusal behaviour* to include all those who refuse to attend school irrespective of the nature or subtype. Hence his work includes populations of children who are not motivated to attend school, such as truants as well as school refusers. He approaches the problem from a behavioural perspective and examines the function underlying the behaviour. He advocates a taxonomy of SR based on a *functional* model as opposed to *forms* of SNA which are underpinned by the constellation of symptoms as discussed above (e.g. anxiety or behaviour difficulties). According to this model a functional analysis of the school refusing behaviour yields four possible reasons (Kearney 2001):

1. Avoidance of negative emotions (e.g. anxiety, distress, depression)

2. Escape from aversive social situations (e.g. bullying) or evaluative situations (e.g. peer interaction in social anxiety/phobia)

3. Obtaining attention from significant others (e.g. parents)

4. Seeking tangible reinforcement or rewards (e.g. watching television, sleeping).

In behavioural terms the first two of the above conditions provide negative reinforcement or avoidance of something aversive and the latter two situations are positively reinforcing. Kearney has devised a questionnaire, the School Refusal Assessment Scale (SRAS; Kearney 2002), to measure the relative strengths of the four functional conditions for a particular case of SR behaviour. The revised form of the scale consists of two versions, SRAS-P for parents and SRAS-C for the youths. The parent version consists of 24 items divided equally across the four functional areas, which are scored on a Likert-type scale of 0 (never) to 6 (always). Negatively reinforced SR behaviour (functions 1 and 2) is largely associated with emotional symptoms like anxiety while the positively reinforced SR behaviour (functions 3 and 4) is associated with behaviour difficulties and conduct problems. The instrument is said to be psychometrically sound with reasonably good reliability.

In his most recent study, which included 222 youths aged 5–17 years, Kearney (2007) has demonstrated that assessing the function of the behaviour using the SRAS was a better determinant of the *degree* of school absenteeism than the form of SR as measured by various questionnaires used to assess forms of psychological disorders such as anxiety and depression. From these findings he concludes that 'examining the function of school refusal behaviour may be a useful adjunct to examining the forms of school refusal behaviour when considering a youth's degree of school absenteeism'. He recommends that a 'comprehensive assessment process that that covers both form *and* function of school refusal behaviour will likely provide the clinician with substantial information that can be directly linked to highly individualized and effective treatment plan' (Kearney 2007). Though the study is methodologically sound, what it demonstrates is rather limited. The main finding of the study is that the function of the behaviour (positive or negative reinforcement) predicts the *duration* of school absenteeism better than identification of the type of SNA.

Kearney's work does not factor in issues such as family dynamics, school environment and individual parental difficulties and is mainly child centred. In practice, however, the practitioner does not work on the basis of the type of SR behaviour alone but takes into consideration a whole host of child, family and school factors that contribute to it. Unfortunately Kearney's study did not take the formulation of the SNA problems into consideration. Nonetheless, an examination of the factors that perpetuate the problem through positive and negative reinforcement has its merits and Kearney's work has made a valuable contribution to the management of what he calls SR behaviour. It must again be pointed out that Kearny's functional model is not specific to SR and is equally applicable to all forms of

SNA including truancy. The model provides a theoretically sound framework for those working in the educational sector and SRAS deserves to be popularised.

Management

There is general agreement that for optimal outcomes the treatment of anxiety-based SR should be mutimodal (American Academy of Child and Adolescent Psychiatry 2007) and that the involvement of the parents and school is essential in order to derive the maximum benefits of treatment. Intervention studies in SR have relied mostly on case reports. A number of theoretical approaches have been employed. Psychodynamic methods of treatment with their underpinnings in mother–child separation difficulties have fallen out of favour, partly because they did not focus sufficiently on return to school and might have inadvertently promoted regression.

Other methods of untested interventions are school counselling, rapid and forced return to school, group therapy and general support for the child at school. In general, behavioural approaches have enjoyed more success than other forms of treatment. Behavioural programmes are based on the principle of systemic desensitisation through graded exposure (see Chapter 5). Although a number of case studies have shown behavioural methods to be effective, there are no methodologically sound or rigorously controlled studies to support their efficacy.

More recently cognitive behavioural therapy (CBT) has been used with clinical populations of school refusers and been reported to be effective. There is growing evidence that cognitive behavioural approaches based primarily on exposure-based interventions together with correction of distorted thinking patterns in these youths are becoming the treatment of choice. Two well-designed studies attest to the efficacy of cognitive-behavioural interventions for school refusers. King *et al.*'s (1998) study involved 34 school refusers aged 5 to 15 years. Diagnostic evaluation showed that 84 per cent experienced a current anxiety or phobic disorder. They were randomly assigned to either a four-week cognitive-behavioural intervention involving gradual return to school and CBT involving six sessions with the child and five with the family; one session was held with the teacher to explain the strategy and enlist corporation. The control group was placed on the waiting list. Relative to controls, the treatment group demonstrated significantly improvement in school attendance (90%), anxiety, fear and coping. Treatment gains were maintained at follow up three months later.

In the second study, Last, Hansen and Franco (1998) randomly allocated 56 school-refusing children to either 12 weeks of CBT or an 'educational and support treatment' group. The CBT treatment consisted of gradual return to school (exposure) and CBT while the latter consisted of manual-based group sessions in which, in addition to providing information to help themselves, children were encouraged to talk about their fears and anxieties and maintain daily diaries. *Both* treatment groups showed clinically and statistically significant levels of improvement and the gains were maintained two weeks into the next school year. Two conclusions may be drawn from these studies: 1. CBT is an effective form of intervention in anxiety-based SR; 2. Educational supportive measures may be equally effective, but the 'active ingredient' in the latter group remains unknown. Despite these finding the potential of educational interventions remains unknown or unreported. As for CBT it should be noted that the trials were small and the drop-out rates were high. In spite of the current popularity of CBT approaches, the evidence on which claims are made is rather limited.

Although there is general agreement that parental involvement is essential in the management of SR, there are no studies that have addressed the role of family interventions. The utility of the functional model of SR behaviour is appealing but its applicability to SR remains unclear. One other consistent finding in research has been that, despite the relentless search for medication to treat SR, the results have been disappointing. For example, a well-designed study failed to show any benefits of medication (in this case Fluoxeine) in separation anxiety disorder (Birmher, Axelson, Monk *et al.* 2003).

In conclusion, current scientific evidence for the effectiveness of most forms of intervention is rather mixed; of these CBT seems to have most support. An authoritative review on the subject concluded, 'Knowledge of "what works" has been built up largely on the basis of clinical experience, and substantial, scientifically sound, controlled studies of treatment efficacy continue to be absent from literature' (Ellis 1999). As a final point on treatment efficacy it should be pointed out that lack of evidence to prove the efficacy of a method of intervention is not evidence of lack of its effectiveness. A method of treatment may be effective but may not have been researched sufficiently or may not lend itself to research. For example, there are no studies to show that using a parachute saves lives when jumping off a plane! On the other hand a highly effective treatment may work only under 'laboratory conditions' in selected populations and be of little use in real-life situations.

Prognosis

In the short term the main consequence of SR is loss of education and associated social isolation. A significant minority of school refusers avoid contact with other children and rapidly come to be confined to the house. This problem has been called 'home bound school absence' (Berg 1992). Most studies show the following to be poor prognostic factors: onset of adolescence, severe symptoms of anxiety, especially social anxiety, and prolonged school absence. SR among primary school children seems to have a better prognosis than in the older age group. Crucial for management is the finding that shorter the duration of refusal the better the outcome. Thus systems for early identification of SR are central to prevention and management.

Long-term follow-up studies of clinical samples show that about one-third of anxious school refusers continue to have emotional and social problems as adults. One of the longest follow-up studies was carried out in Sweden. This study followed 35 school refusers for 20 to 29 years. All 35 children were diagnosed which separation anxiety when they were 7–12 years old. Their outcome was compared with two groups of similar numbers of age and sex-matched children from the general population and non-school refusing psychiatric patients. The study showed that as adults the school refuser group: (1) had significantly more psychiatric consultation (30% compared with 10% in controls); (2) tended to live with their parents (10% compared with 0%); and (3) had fewer children than the comparison groups (70% compared with 45%) (Flakierska-Praquin, Lindstrom and Gillberg 1997). Similar findings were reported in a study that followed up 168 secondary school-age children who had been admitted to a psychiatric inpatient unit on account of severe SR. Ten years after discharge (mean age 24 years), a third had received treatment for psychiatric illnesses and 5 per cent had been admitted to a psychiatric ward. At the time of follow up one-third of the sample reported minor psychiatric disability including anxiety and depression (Berg and Jackson 1985). These and other studies confirm that, as a group, children with SR tend to suffer in later life from anxiety and/or depression and find independent living difficult.

A negative finding worth pointing out is that studies have now conclusively shown that SR is a not a precursor of agoraphobia in later adulthood. Agoraphobia is an anxiety disorder in which the subject experiences extreme anxiety about being in situations from which escape might difficult (or embarrassing) such as being out of the home alone or being in a crowd. Earlier workers had postulated that given the similarity between SR in childhood and agoraphobia in adults, that SR developed into agoraphobia when the children grew up. This has been shown not to be the case (King *et al.* 1998).

Conclusions

Taken as a whole, over the last few decades a respectable body of research on the subject of SR has accumulated, although there remain large gaps in our knowledge on the issue. A number of scholarly books are now available as well as treatment manuals based on sound theoretical principles. It is now possible to make a number of assertions based on research evidence and the chapters in this book are based on the best available evidence. However, there are methodological and theoretical barriers in researching this field. For example, the lack of proper and inclusive operational criteria to define SR in research has been a major obstacle to drawing conclusions and generalisations from studies. Recent work by Kearney and colleagues has confused the issues further by using SR *behaviour* as the focus of study. Moreover, there are hardly any standardised instruments or rating scaled which measure SR. No field of inquiry can expect to make progress unless there are reliable and valid measures for its identification. As pointed out at the beginning of the chapter the vast majority of the research carried out on SR has been on selected populations typically those presenting to child mental health clinics. Hardly any studies have been conducted with the whole range of school refusers as seen by those in the frontline.

It is important to point out that in day-to-day practice one is guided by a judicious combination of general psychological principles, experience and a large measure of common sense as well as the available of scientific evidence. While academics and researchers need to research the subject more rigorously, practitioners need to be able to utilise whatever research findings are available and apply them in their day-to-day practice. As pointed out above, absence of evidence is not evidence of absence.

Appendix II Specimen Assessment Form

Name:

Date of birth (age):

School:

Grade:

School non-attendance difficulties and history (duration and pattern of school refusal, continuous /non-continuous absence, other difficulties, reasons given for non-attendance):

School/educational history (past school attendance difficulties, change of schools, present difficulties including attendance records, academic ability, recent test results, possible learning difficulties or difficulties with specific subjects or teachers, change in groups, possible bullying):

Family (composition, family tree (genogram), recent changes in family circumstances, family stresses, and other problems in family, e.g. anxiety/ depression in parents, parents' beliefs about the reason for the problem):

Significant developmental and medical history (developmental milestones and any setbacks, past and present physical illness in the child, medically sanctioned absences):

Child interview (child's view of difficulties, typical day, presence of features of anxiety, separation difficulties social anxieties, fear thermometer, hobbies, interests, what he or she misses most about school, difficulties with lessons/teachers):

School report and meeting/liaison with teachers (record of attendance, possible bullying, teachers views about behaviour, peer relationships, general ability, strengths and difficulties, learning sets, results of SATs, on the SEN register?, help available at school):

Other professionals involved (EWO, SHA, EP, home tuition services, CAMHS, SENCo, social worker; their respective roles):

Integration of information and formulation (hypotheses) (family, child and school factors contributing to school problem; see Figure 4.5):

Appendix 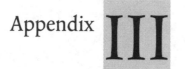 Handout for Parents

What is school refusal?

Quite a few children will, at some point, be very reluctant to go to school or even refuse to go to school. This can cause serious problems. If your child misses a lot of school, their education may be badly affected. Absence from school may undermine their confidence and impair peer relationships and impede their social development as they grow up. Legally, parents are responsible for making sure that their child is educated. The term *school refusal* refers to difficulties that some children show in attending school and is usually due to anxiety and worry the child may be experiencing. This has sometimes been called 'school phobia'. It is very different from truancy, where the child keeps away from school without the knowledge of parents; this often happens in the context of other behaviour problems such as disruptive behaviour at school, aggression, fighting with other children and other antisocial behaviours.

In school refusal the child is usually too anxious to go to school. Refusal to go to school may begin following a period at home in which the child has become closer to the parent, such as a holiday break or a brief illness. It also may follow a stressful occurrence, such as the death of a pet or relative, a change of schools or a move to a new school. Worrying about going to school can make them feel vaguely unwell, with sickness, headaches, tummy aches, poor appetite and frequent visits to the toilet, although usually no physical cause can be found for these symptoms. The symptoms are usually worse on weekday mornings and tend to disappear later in the day. A child may seem to be worried about going to school, when actually they are fearful about leaving the safety of their home and parents or interacting with peers at school. However, once they are in school and get involved in lessons and seeing their friends, they may find that they enjoy school.

Anxiety

All children (and adults) experience some anxiety in their everyday lives. Anxiety in children is expected and normal at specific times in development. For example, from approximately eight months through the preschool years, healthy youngsters may show intense distress (anxiety) at times of separation from their parents or other persons to whom they are close. Anxious children are often overly tense or uptight. Some may seek a lot of reassurance, and their worries may interfere with their activities. Because anxious children may also be quiet, compliant and eager to please, their difficulties may be missed. Parents should be alert to the signs of severe anxiety so they can intervene early to prevent complications. Sometimes the anxiety is associated with separation from parents and at other times it is associated with fear of interacting with peers and other people. The former is called separation anxiety and the latter social anxiety.

Features of separation anxiety include:

- constant thoughts and intense fears about the safety of parents and caretakers

- refusing to go to school

- frequent stomach aches and other physical complaints

- extreme worries about sleeping away from home

- being overly clingy

- panic or tantrums at times of separation from parents

- trouble sleeping or nightmares.

Characteristics of social anxiety include:

- fear of meeting or talking to people

- avoidance of social situations

- few friends outside the family

- the fears cause significant distress and interfere with usual activities.

Other features of anxious children include:

- worries about things before they happen

- constant worries or concerns about family, school, friends, or activities

- repetitive, unwanted thoughts (obsessions) or actions (compulsions)

- fears of embarrassment or making mistakes

- low self-esteem and lack of self-confidence.

What causes school refusal?

Usually there is no single 'cause' for school refusal. Family problems and school difficulties may play a part. In young children a change in the family, even the birth of a younger brother or sister, may be enough to upset them. There may be other reasons – illness in a parent, arguments or a death in the family. Some children are more prone to be anxious and worried and particularly vulnerable. Bullying at school and problems with school work or with teachers and peers are also common reasons that contribute to the difficulties.

Where to get help and what can be done

If your child is not going to school, they need to be able to talk to you and their teachers about any worries they might have. Make sure that they know you are there to support them. This will help them to know that their problems are being taken seriously. Children themselves need to be involved in planning how best to overcome these problems.

You and your child's teachers should encourage your child to go back to school *as quickly as possible*. Keeping your child off school will make the problem worse. If you sort out any underlying problems, like bullying or difficulties with school work, many of the symptoms will improve.

Parents and teachers need to work with the child to get them back into school as quickly as possible. Underlying problems, such as reading or other academic difficulties, may need special help. Where there is a possibility that the child is being subjected to bullying, this needs to be addressed with the school. Parents and teachers will need to keep an eye on whether the child is actually attending school. They should make sure that they reward the child for any improvements in their attendance.

General management and advice to parents and carers

- If you feel the physical symptoms are due to a physical illness you should seek a medical opinion as soon as possible. Once physical causes have been excluded, rapid return to school is important.

- Explore with the child the source of the child's anxieties about attending school/leaving home, and deal with these as far as possible.

The following steps will enable many children to return to school successfully:

- Establish an agreement for the goal of the child's return to school.

- Form close links with a key member of the school staff to work out and support school return plans and deal with issues such as bullying or academic difficulties.

- The child's return to school may need to be in small steps with consolidation of success at each stage. It is essential to set realistic targets and closely monitor progress.

- The plans usually involve parents taking the child to school until confidence is restored; the father's involvement in this is often crucial to success.

- Parents should take a firm and consistent line over keeping to the return to school plans. There may be an upsurge of distress from their child to start with, which needs to be managed calmly, and praise given when the child succeeds.

- Arrange for a safe haven in school for the child where he or she can go to if he or she becomes very distressed in class; avoid picking up the child when he or she complains of excessive distress while in school.

- Once the child is back in school, anticipate a recurrence of some anxiety about returning to school after holidays or illnesses. Preparing for such eventualities is important to ensure the attendance problem does not recur.

In severe and long-standing school refusal, a pupil referral unit may provide a valuable halfway house between school and the social isolation of staying at home that is more acceptable to the young person than returning to a large school. Home tutors can play a useful role with persistent school refusers by helping them to make the transition between home and school, or between home and tutorial unit, then tutorial unit and school.

Dos...

- Once agreed, try to adhere to the return to school plan. Accept no excuse for not going to school.

- Parents need to work together and agree on a joint approach to their child's difficulties.

- Take a firm and consistent approach; set firm rules and get the child to school every morning.

- Be prepared to place reasonable pressure on the child and push the child to the point of mild panic when urging the child to go to school; ignore threats and screams.

- Present a (parental) united front.

- Support the partner who is entrusted with taking the child to school especially during the initial period of the return to school plan; be prepared to take time off work during the early stages of the implementation of the plan

- If for whatever reason, the child does not make it in the morning he or she should be made to go after a period of settling down.

- Contact the allocated teacher or key worker everyday to ensure that the plan is working.

- Be prepared to manage your own anxieties and reservations without discussing them with the child; keep parental issues separate from child issues.

- Discuss any related adult/parental problems with the appropriate professionals.

- Praise the child for adhering to the plan; give credit to the child (rather than to the plan).

- Be prepared to tolerate anxiety symptoms the child may complain of (abdominal pain, diarrhoea, etc.).

- Make sure both parents spend protected time with the child independent of the school attendance problems; do not make the school refusal problem the main topic of your conversation at home.

- When the child is not at school (or in home tuition) get the child to adhere to a set timetable for the day that includes getting up from bed in time and study hours.

- It is crucially important for there to be good communication with the school.

And Don'ts...

- Don't provide excuses for the child to remain at home; it merely intensifies the problems.

- Don't allow your anxieties and worries get in the way of the return to school plan; discuss them with your partner and the professionals involved.

- Don't let the child see any of your doubts or worries; keep it within the adult system.

- Don't let the child watch TV, play computer programmes or enjoy other activities when he or she is at home during school hours not and not at school. Create an atmosphere of 'solitary confinement' as long as the child is at home.

- Don't seek repeated medical advice for the child for minor ailments or give non-prescription drugs for the child's physical complaints.

- Don't criticise school or teachers in the presence of the child; remember that children are clever at picking up non-verbal cues and a mere look of disapproval of some aspect of school will be capitalised on by the child.

- Don't change school. It is usually unhelpful because the problems tend to recur in the new setting.

Recommended reading and sources of information

C.A. Kearney and A.N. Albano (2004) *When Children Refuse School: A Cognitive Behavioural Therapy Approach:Therapist Guide.* San Antonio, TX: Psychological Corporation.
A simple workbook for parents based on Kearney's model.

R. Rapee, S. Spence, V. Cobham and A. Wignall (2000) *Helping Your Anxious Child: A Step- by-Step Guide for Parents.* Oakland, CA: New Harbinger Publications.
A practical guidebook for parents, more suitable for the primary school child.

Advisory Centre for Education (ACE)
0808 800 5793
Website: http://www.ace-ed.org.uk
A general advice line and independent advice centre for parents, offering free advice on many topics including exclusion from school, bullying, special educational needs and school admission appeals.

Young Minds Parent information line
Tel: 0800 018 2138
Website: http://www.youngminds.org.uk
Produces books and leaflets about young people's mental health and offers seminars and training.

Parent Partnership Services
Website: www.parentpartnership.org
Parent partnership services are statutory services that offer information, advice and support for parents of children and young people with special educational needs (SEN). They will also be able to put parents in touch with other local organisations. PPSs also have a role in making sure that the parents' views are heard and understood and that these views inform local policy and practice. Most parent partnerships are based in their LEA (Local Education Authority) or Children's Trust.

References

American Academy of Child and Adolescent Psychiatry (2007) 'Practice parameter for the assessment and treatment of children and adolescents with anxiety disorders.' *Journal of the American Academy of Child and Adolescent Psychiatry 46*, 267–283.

Archer, T., Filmer-Sankey, C. and Fletcher-Campbell, F. (2003) *School Phobia and School Refusal: Research into Causes and Remedies. LGA Research Report 46.* Slough: NFER.

Atkinson, M. and Hornby, G. (2002) *Mental Health Handbook for Schools.* Oxford: Routledge/Falmer.

Atkinson, L., Quarrington, B. and Cyr, J. J. (1985) 'School refusal: the heterogeneity of a concept.' *American Journal of Orthopsychiatry 5*, 83–101.

Audit Commission (1999) *Missing Out: LEA Management of School Attendance and Exclusion.* London: Audit Commission.

Beidel, D.C., Turner, S.M. and Morris, T.L. (1999) 'Psychopathology of childhood social phobia.' *Journal of the American Academy of Child and Adolescent Psychiatry 38*, 643–650.

Berg, I. (1992) 'Absence from school and mental health.' *British Journal of Psychiatry 161*, 154–156.

Berg, I. and Jackson, A. (1985) 'Teenage school refusers grow up: follow up study of 168 subjects ten years on average after in-patient treatment.' *British Journal of Psychiatry 147*, 366–370.

Berg, I., Butler, A., Franklin, J., Hays, H., Lucas, C. and Sims, R. (1993) 'DSM – III- R disorders, social factors and management of school attendance problems in the normal population.' *Journal of Child Psychology and Psychiatry 34*, 1187–1203.

Berg, I., Butler, A., Franklin, I. and McGuire, R. (1981) 'The parents of school phobic adolescents.' *Psychological Medicine 11*, 79–83.

Berg, I., Nichols, K. and Prichard, C. (1969) 'School phobia – its classification and its relationship to dependency.' *Journal of Child and Psychology and Psychiatry 10*, 123–141.

Bion, W.R. (1963) *Elements of Psychoanalysis.* London: Heinemann.

Birmher, B., Axelson, D.A., Monk, K. *et al.* (2003) 'Fluoxetine for the treatment of school refusal.' *Journal of the American Academy of Child and Adolescent Psychiatry 42*, 415–423.

Bools, C., Foster, J., Brown, I. and Berg, I. (1990) 'The identification of psychiatric disorders in children who fail to attend school: a cluster analysis of a non-clinical population.' *Psychological Medicine 20*, 171–181.

Broadwin, I.T. (1932) 'A contribution to the study of truancy.' *American Journal of Orthopsychiatry 2*, 253–259.

Cicchetti, D., Toth, S.L. and Maughan, A. (2000) 'An Ecological-Transactional Model of Child Maltreatment.' In A. J. Sameroff, M. Lewis and S. M. Miller (eds) *Handbook of Developmental Psychopathology*, 2nd edn. New York: Kluwer Academic/ Plenum Publishers.

Crick, N.R. and Grotpeter, J.K. (1992) 'Children's treatment by peers: victims of relational and overt aggression.' *Developmental Psychopathology 8*, 367–380.

DfES (2000) *Access to Education for Children and Young People with Medical Needs.* London: Stationery Office.

DfES (2002) 'Discipline in schools: secretary of state's speech 12 December 2002 to social market foundation.' London: Stationery Office.

DfES (2003) *Every Child Matters: Change for Children.* London: Stationery Office.

DfES (2006) Pupil absence in schools in England 2005/2006. FR35/2006. Avialable at: www.dfes.gov.uk/rsgateway/DB/SFR/S000679/ index.shtml (accessed 23 October 2007)..

Department for Education and Employment (1999) *Tackling Truancy Together: A Strategy Document.* London: DfEE.

Department for Education and Employment (2000) *Social Inclusion: Pupil Support Briefing*, vol. 2, Spring. London: DfEE.

Dowling, E. and Osborne, E. (1994) *The Family and the School: A Joint Systems Approach to Problems with Children*, 2nd edn. London: Routledge.

Egger, H.L., Costello, E.J. and Angold, A. (2003) 'School refusal and psychiatric disorders: a community study.' *Journal of the American Academy of Child and Adolescent Psychiatry 42*, 797–807.

Ellis, J.G. (1999) 'Practitioner review: school refusal: issues of conceptualisation, assessment and treatment.' *Journal of Child Psychology and Psychiatry 40*, 7, 1001–1012.

Flakierska-Praquin, N., Lindstrom, M. and Gillberg, C. (1997) 'School phobia with separation anxiety disorder: a comparative 20–29-year follow-up study of 35 school refusers.' *Comparative Psychiatry 38*, 17–22.

Fogelman, K., Tibbenham, A. and Lambert, I. (1980) 'Absence from School: Findings from The National Child Developmental Study.' In L. Hersov and I. Berg (eds) *Out of School – Modern Perspectives in Truancy and School Refusal.* Chichester: John Wiley.

Freydenberg, E. and Lewis, R. (1993) *The Adolescent Coping Scale – Administrator's Manual.* Melbourne: Australian Council for Educational Research.

Gardner, R. (1992) 'Children with Separation Anxiety Disorder.' In J. D. O'Brian, D. J. Pilowsky and O.W. Lewis (eds) *Psychotherapies with Children and Adolescents: Adapting the Psychodynamic Process.* Washington, DC: American Psychiatric Press.

Graham, P. (2005) (ed.) *Cognitive Behaviour Therapy for Children and Families*, 2nd edn. Oxford: Oxford University Press. (Chapter 19 deals with school refusal.)

Granell de Aldaz, R., Vivas, E., Gelfand, D.M. and Feldman, L. (1984) 'Estimating the prevalence of school refusal and school-related fears: a Venezuelan sample.' *Journal of Mental and Nervous Diseases 172*, 722–729.

Hampe, E., Miller, L., Barrett, C. and Noble, H. (1973) 'Intelligence and school phobia.' *Journal of School Psychology 11*, 66–70.

Hersov, L.A. (1977) 'School Refusal.' In M. Rutter and L.A. Hersov (eds.) *Child Psychiatry: Modern Approaches.* Oxford: Blackwell.

Johnson, A.M., Falstein, E.I. and Szureck, S.A. (1941) 'School phobia.' *American Journal of Orthopsychiatry 11*, 702–711.

Kearney, C.A. (2001) *School Refusal Behaviour in Youth: A Functional Approach to Assessment and Treatment.* Washington, DC: American Psychological Association.

Kearney, C.A. (2002) 'Identifying the function of school refusal behaviour: a revision of the School Refusal Assessment Scale.' *Journal of Psychopathology and Behavioral Assessment 24*, 235–245.

Kearney, C.A. (2007) 'Forms and functions of school refusal behavior in youth: an empirical analysis of absenteeism severity.' *Journal of Child Psychology and Psychiatry 48*, 53–61.

Kearney, C.A. and Silverman, W.K. (1995) 'Family environment of youngsters with school refusal behaviour: a synopsis with implications for assessment and treatment.' *American Journal of Family Therapy 23*, 59–72.

King, N.J. and Bernstein, G.A. (2001) 'School refusal in children and adolescents: a review of past 10 years.' *Journal of the American Academy of Child and Adolescent Psychiatry 40*, 197–205

King, N.J., Tonge, B.J., Heyne, B.J., Prichard, M., Rollings, S., Young, D., Myerson, N. and Ollendick, T.H. (1998) 'Cognitive-behavioural treatment of school-refusing children: a controlled evaluation.' *Journal of the American Academy of Child and Adolescent Psychiatry 37*, 395–403.

Last, C.G., Hansen, M.S. and Franco, N. (1998) 'Cognitive–behavioral treatment of school phobia.' *Journal of the American Academy of Child and Adolescent Psychiatry 37*, 4, 404–411.

Last, C.G. and Strauss, C.C. (1990) 'School refusal in anxiety disordered children and adolescents.' *Journal of the American Academy of Child and Adolescent Psychiatry 37*, 404–411.

Marks, I. (1969) *Fears and Phobias.* London: Heineman.

Meikle, J. (2006) 'One pupil in five plays truant, new figures show.' The Guardian, 22 September.

Mental Health Foundation (1999) *Bright Futures: Promoting Children and Young People's Mental Health.* London: The Mental Health Foundation.

National Association of Chief Education Welfare Officers (1975) *These We Serve: A Report of a Working Party Set up to Enquire into the Causes of Absence from School.* Bedford: NACEWO.

O'Keeffe, D. and Stoll, P. (1995) *School Attendance and Truancy: Understanding and Management of the Problem.* London: Pitman Publishing.

Ollendick, T.H. and Mayer, J.A. (1984) 'School phobia.' In S.M. Turner (ed.) *Behavioural Theories and Treatment of Anxiety.* New York: Plenum. (pp.36–411).

Olweus, D. (1993) *Bullying at School: What We Know and We Can Do.* Oxford: Blackwell.

Olweus, D. (1994) 'Annotation: Bullying at school: Basic facts and effects of a school based intervention program.' *Journal of Child Psychology and Psychiatry 35*, 1171–1190.

Plas, J. (1986) *Systems Psychology in the Schools.* New York: Pergamon Press.

Roeser, R.W. and Eccles, J. S. (2000) 'Schooling and Mental Health.' In A. J. Sameroff, M. Lewis and S. M. Miller (eds) *Handbook of Developmental Psychopathology*, 2nd edn. New York: Kluwer Academic/ Plenum Publishers.

Thambirajah, M.S. (2004) *The Psychological Basis of Psychiatry*. Edinburgh: Churchill Livingstone.

West Sussex County Council Educational Psychology Service (2004) *Emotionally Based School Refusal: Guidance for Schools and Support Agencies*. West Sussex County Council EPS.

Subject Index

Author Index